A SONG IS RISING

Reigniting the Warrior Within

Wendy Parker

D.o.l.l.
MINISTRIES

www.dollministries.com
Adelaide, South Australia
info@dollministries.com

© Wendy Parker 2023

ISBN: 978-0-6455086-7-3

All rights reserved. Except for private study, research, criticism or reviews, as permitted under the Copyright Act, no part of this book may be reproduced, stored in a retrieval system, or transmitted in any form or by any means without prior written permission. Enquiries should be made to the publisher.

Publisher's Note: This is a work of non-fiction. Names of persons have been used with permission.

Cataloguing-in-Publications entry is available from the National Library of Australia http:/catalogue.nla.gov.au

Quotes from the Bible are referenced at the conclusion of each chapter.
Referenced scripture taken from the New King James Version®. Copyright © 1982 by Thomas Nelson. Used by permission. All rights reserved.
Referenced scripture taken from The Voice™. Copyright © 2012 by Ecclesia Bible Society. Used by permission. All rights reserved.
Referenced scriptures taken from the Holy Bible, New International Version®, NIV®. Copyright © 1973, 1978, 1984, 2011 by Biblica, Inc.™ Used by permission of Zondervan. All rights reserved worldwide. www.zondervan.com The "NIV" and "New International Version" are trademarks registered in the United States Patent and Trademark Office by Biblica, Inc.™
Referenced scripture taken from the Amplified Bible, Copyright © 2015 by The Lockman Foundation. Used by permission.
Referenced scripture quotations are from The Passion Translation®. Copyright © 2017, 2018, 2020 by Passion & Fire Ministries, Inc. Used by permission. All rights reserved. ThePassionTranslation.com.

Cover and author photo by Lauren Parker

First edition published 2023

'This book is a timely reminder for all Christians to stand tall as warriors, and in Wendy's words, to "stop playing it small. Stop hiding in the shadows that incarcerate and confine you because your liberation will liberate others."
A thought provoking read.'

Carolyn Miller, bestselling Australian author of
the Regency Wallflowers and Original Six series.

'Wendy Parker doesn't just write books, she invites us into her loungeroom, offers us a cup of tea and gives a good pep talk. A Song is Rising is a beautifully written book full of biblical examples and raw personal stories that speaks to the struggles many of us face, whilst simultaneously reminding us of a God who is bigger than our fears and insecurities. By the time you have finished reading, you'll have a blueprint when facing any challenge that comes your way and what it takes to re-awaken the warrior within you'

Nicole Partridge, journalist and writer

For my three warriors
Philip, Samuel, and Lauren.

'We've passed through fire and flood,
yet in the end you always bring us
out better than we were before,
saturated with your goodness.'
Psalm 66: 12 (TPT)

FOREWORD

When the Lord whispered *'arise'* in my spirit, I never imagined it would be an idea for me to keep warm for a season before passing the mantle on. I did know, however, that Wendy had a role to play in it.

Whatever *it* was.

Together, Wendy and I excitedly dreamed of co-authoring a non-fiction project. However, as the months went by, the Lord called me back to my fiction roots, while He simultaneously stirred Wendy's heart with visions of the Phoenix and Miriam. Fire and water. Thus, 'arise' transferred from my open hands into Wendy's, where it would thrive.

In a way only God could orchestrate—and completely unbeknownst to either of us at the beginning—I became Wendy's target audience. Her avatar. Every chapter written under dictation of the Holy Spirit both challenged and inspired me.

Neither of us saw it coming but somehow every spiritual attack against my calling was countered by the power-packed arsenal compiled in this book. As Wendy writes, 'God is able to take the smallest of sparks and ignite something good.' Only the Lord knew what I would need to rise and reignite the warrior within me. And as it turns out, it would take fire and water.

In her book *The Way of Perfection*, St Teresa of Avila writes, 'the fire and the water are not contraries, but have the same origin. Do not fear that the one element may harm the other; each helps the other and they produce the same effect.'

When I think of water, I imagine a tranquil space, ebbing and flowing with freedom of thought and creativity. In contrast, I consider fire to be the burning in my soul when I am inspired and ignited for God and His Word. In these fiery moments, my mouth often can't keep up with the swelling of my heart and mind as I grasp gifted concepts from the King of Heaven Himself. I feel on fire from the inside out.

But what does it look like to feel like water? What would it be like for the peace of God to saturate my soul and transform me through divine osmosis?

Fire and water—though typically competing elements—can work together in harmony. One supports the other in the environment that is our souls. Like bushfires that prepare the ground and the rain that brings new life, these elements come in waves and seasons. But, as you will discover in this book, fire and water can also come at once in a rising storm of divine inspiration that will reignite the warrior within, guiding us deeper into our calling and giving us the courage to rise in song and proclaim the transforming power of Jesus Christ.

Elizabeth Chapman,
author and founder of DOLL Ministries

A LETTER TO THE READER

After my first book, *Wounded And On The Run: How Your Worst Pain Can lead You Into Your Greatest Calling* was released, testimonies from my readers revealed how much they had found healing from the wounds they had carried. However, it was the little wooden cabin in the forest readers fondly spoke of and how it had created a safe place for rest and recovery from the wounds of each disappointment and painful memory that had left a blood trail behind them. And it was only then I came to realise that the cabin I had created for my readers, the safe space that had been assembled from my own wounding and pain, the cabin that had been formed and fashioned for the broken-hearted to discover the transformational power found in the victorious scars on the hands and feet of Jesus, a sacred space that protected and shielded the wounded from the arrows of affliction and bullets of shame that the hunter, Satan so readily fires was possibly the start of something good. This safe place shaped by Jesus' own wounds revealed a part of us that we, the wounded ones, had kept hidden for far too long.

Many wounded souls were so impacted by the elk analogy and how it applies to their own blood trailing, that they asked if I was going to write a sequel that was like a follow-up shot, so to speak. Something they were able to aim at the hunter, Satan that could slow him down in the chase. A weapon that made sure he wouldn't be able to reload his bow or rifle so easily this time and take aim at their fresh scars causing old wounds to seep back into a blood trail that kept them running.

To be honest, I wasn't planning to write a follow-on book, an essential shot that took down the enemy because I felt my first book was a powerful, stand-alone message that required no follow-up shot. Why would my readers need a follow-up when they had become equipped with God's armour? They understood the redeeming power found in the scars of Jesus, they had discovered each one of the hunter's schemes, surely they felt bold and courageous enough to move beyond the safety of the little wooden cabin in the forest and rise up, ready to lead others to the One who had been wounded first. Right?

Perhaps.

Nevertheless, it was time for readers to move on to the next part of the journey and leave me to welcome others into the little wooden cabin for their much-needed healing. And despite the fact we had hugged and said our goodbyes outside the narrow cabin door, the one with the window boxes full of brightly coloured flowers that represented the saints who had marched in before us, a great cloud of witnesses cheering us all on as found in Hebrews 12:1-2, it was now time for readers to look forward to what lay ahead and to not look back because each wound had indeed turned into a victorious scar.

But you did look back, dear reader, and you whispered a question that clung so tightly to the crisp morning air that I could reach out my hand and grab it. You said, *'What do I do now?'*

And as you exhaled, the question lingered between us in the foggy vapour that had risen from your lips as your eyes met mine and they told me not to abandon you when this was possibly the moment you needed my help the most. And as I stood there on the cabin steps watching you head toward the many paths that would lead you to the edge of the forest, it was the question, the look back, the anguish in your eyes as you picked at your fresh scars, that I felt the pang of abandonment I knew so well. And it is that moment that has haunted my soul and hounded me relentlessly.

'What do I do now?' It's a question we often ask when we look at our fresh scars. The lines that frame our stories of what we've been through. And yet we still wonder if we will ever be able to be truly free as we try to find the courage to rise up from the ashes of our past and move forward into an unknown future. One thing is clear though, dear friend, you're not who you were when you first found the little wooden cabin hidden deep within the forest where your wounds were cleansed and healed so gently by Jesus Himself. Let me encourage, by reminding you that you have enough knowledge now to understand that the scars we all carry are only a chapter in our stories and not the whole book.

However, it was the look back you gave me, that was the moment, I believe, where we both suddenly realised something. We realised each scar that carried our stories was what had connected us to each other in the first place. A collective group of overcomers who had now found themselves standing in the in between and saying to each other, 'What do I do now?' We knew in that moment that something had indeed changed on the inside of us, and now, together, we wanted to know where to go from here. As Kris Vallotton points out, 'most of us don't even know who we are, because we haven't stopped long enough to say hello to ourselves… if we don't know who we are or how we are doing, how can we really share ourselves with others?"[1] I totally agree. We, the wounded ones, haven't been able to stop running long enough to say hello to ourselves, so we have forgotten who we are and what we're capable of. In a way, deep wounds cause you to lose yourself, cause you to keep reverting back to staying hidden. I know, you're scared of awakening something inside of you, so you chose to hide instead of rising. Sadly, this is what the hunter, Satan, wants. He wants our voices to stay silent instead of being heard, the wounded ones to stay enslaved by our past, hidden in the ashes of all our fears and anxious thoughts because we've forgotten who we are. So, my dear friend, I want you to know that I have heard your question and I need you to know that I now understand that I *cannot* leave you to fight this war on your own. You need a follow-up shot, one that will help you to rise into the future God has for you and teach you how trust Him completely with every step. And this is the reason why I wrote, *A Song Is Rising: Reigniting The Warrior Within*.

This book is your follow-up shot.

Believe it or not, the hunter, Satan, knew you had this weapon all along. However, he was hoping it would draw a blank in your memory so that it wouldn't cause any damage to his game plan that has kept you down, deterring you, the overcomer from rising. But the thing about this follow-up shot is that it isn't shaped like the hunter's ammunition. No, its powerful aim is far more damaging to our enemy than his poisoned arrow tips and rounds of bullying bullets he continually fires to create a blood trail. It is a secret weapon, one that is designed to enhance and accompany each part of God's armour you found in the pages of *Wounded And On The Run*. This book is a vital piece of weaponry that must be taken on the journey that is ahead of you. A weapon that will be melded and shaped into a song with lyrics to a melody that many have forgotten how to sing. A beat sheet that sets the pace as you forge ahead with each courageous new step that will take you on a journey toward the Living Waters that quenches even the driest of souls.

In Revelation 21:4 it promises that 'the pain of wounds will no longer exist, for the old order has ceased.'[2] So, dear friend, it's time to shake off the ashes of your past mistakes and stop picking at your fresh scars. It is time you discovered the fire that burns within as you journey toward the refreshing fountain that is God's gracious gift to the conquering ones.[3]

INTRODUCTION

In Greek folklore, the Phoenix is a bird that dies in the combustion of flames and is reborn from the ashes. The Phoenix learns to trust the process and purpose of the fire, so it is able to find the courage to rise again. The prophet Isaiah speaks about beauty for ashes. 'God has sent me to give them a beautiful crown in exchange for ashes, to anoint them with gladness instead of sorrow, to wrap them in victory, joy, and praise instead of depression and sadness.'[4]

Are you ready to turn those ashes of your past into something beautiful? I believe this book is going reawaken and reignite the warrior that has been lying dormant within you. But first, I need you to do me one favour. I need you to stop looking back at the cabin in the forest and let 'the Lord guide you continually and satisfy your soul in drought and strengthen your bones, only then will you be like a watered garden and like a spring of water whose waters do not fail.'[5] Looking back will only hinder your progress in finding the Living Water that can flood even the most dehydrated parts of your precious scarred soul with a fountain that flows with the promise of a fresh, new beginning. We will be taking this journey together and it will be no small feat. I would be lying if I didn't tell you that we have a difficult path ahead of us. So, besides me, you're going to need another companion, a trusty guide who can help uncover every trap and peril of what lies ahead. A fellow traveller who will help fan the flames for reignition. So, who could help reignite the warrior within you? Who has the knowledge and skill set that would show you the way? Well, I went on a search to find just the right person, and I believe, I have found a warrior leader who is equipped enough for the job.

Let me introduce, Miriam, the prophetess. Sister to Moses and Aaron and a leader in her own right. She will be our head guide throughout our journey that we are about to embark on. As Miriam takes you by the hand and leads you to the edge of the forest into unknown territory, she will be the trusted friend who will walk you through the process of those first wobbly steps as you start to move beyond the forest boundary line. This brave woman will show you how to fully trust God, even when the path becomes unsteady and uncertain, even when your faith feels like it's being consumed with the searing heat and flames of all your what if and if only questions that can burn up and bury your confidence stopping you from rising into everything God has for your future.

Again, I must stress, for this follow-up shot to be effective, you need to stop looking back at what was, otherwise you'll become paralysed with fear and stay hidden in the ashes forever.

With the help of Miriam's story and leadership insights from my own journey of discovering the warrior within, you'll find that even in the midst of doubts and struggles God is able to take the smallest of sparks and ignite something good.

So, dear friend, are you ready?

Good.

Because it is time to use this follow-up shot, letting the enemy know that the overcomers are ready to rise once again.

Endnotes:

Ref 1   Volloton, Kris, 2014. *Fashioned To Reign: Empowering Women To Fulfill Their Divine Destiny.* Chosen Publishing Group

Ref 2   Revelation 21:4. *The Passion Translation: New Testament with Psalms, Proverbs, and Song of Songs, Second Edition.* Passion & Fire Ministries, Inc. BroadStreet Publishing:2018.

Ref 3   Revelation 21:7. *The Passion Translation: New Testament with Psalms, Proverbs, and Song of Songs, Second Edition.* Passion & Fire Ministries, Inc. BroadStreet Publishing:2018.

Ref 4   Isaiah 61:3. *Spiritual Warfare Bible. 2012. Lake Mary, Florida, Charisma House.*

Ref 5   Isaiah 58:11. *Spiritual Warfare Bible. 2012. Lake Mary, Florida, Charisma House.*

PART ONE

THE EXODUS

CHAPTER ONE

Reigniting The Warrior Within

'I know that strength arising from obedience has a way of simplifying things which seem impossible.'[1]
ST TERESA OF AVILA

'*Who chose you?*' The words were so distinct, so clear that I suddenly became roused and fully awake in the dim light of a fresh, new sunrise that was just starting to peek through my bedroom blinds one summer's morning just before Christmas last year. I knew it was the unmistakable voice of God because my own thoughts hadn't yet kicked into my consciousness. The thoughts that were ready to pick up their conversation from where they'd left off the night before. The ones that had left me drowning in a sea of self-doubt and uncertainty before I had finally given in and fallen into a restless sleep.

I decided to get up and write the words I had audibly heard down on a note card. As I wrote, I whispered, '*You. It was You who chose me, God.'* And as I lay the pen back down, I thought that even though my scars were victorious, even though I had uncovered the hunter's tactics and taught others how to use each piece of God's armour to keep the hunter, Satan, from starting another blood trail, I still battled with a deep insecurity that God was going to take me so far into my journey of what He had called me to do and leave me there. Not only leave me drowning in that moment, but let me down, disappoint me, and dare I say it, abandon me completely. Where were these thoughts coming from? Nevertheless, the words I had heard reverberated with the ones found in John 15:16 as Jesus reminds His disciples that 'you have not chosen Me, but I have chosen you and I have appointed and placed and purposefully planted you.'[2]

Did you get that message loud and clear, Satan? God *chose* me.

I am appointed, placed, and purposefully planted.

And let me remind you dear friend, if you've had doubts circling your thoughts as to whether God chose you, I assure you today, that God truly, completely, and unmistakably has *chosen you*. The Eternal One who promises never to abandon us (Deuteronomy 31:6) was reminding this weary warrior drowning in her thoughts and questioning that He doesn't make mistakes in His choosing.

Let me say that again.

God DOES NOT make mistakes!

Clearly, my first book had caused our adversary to become so enraged, by helping wounded people, that it had forced him to change up his game plan. He had drawn up new blueprints in the battle for my mind now that his old schemes and plans had been exposed. Believe me when I tell you, he is relentless in hunting us down because together we, the overcomers, have taken much of his territory by using God's armour and he is aiming his arrows specifically at our scars.

Why?

Because the target of the adversary's fiery darts is to poke and point at your freshly healed wounds as he desires to cause them to blister and welt, leaving a blood trail that will flow behind you once again. His attack this time? To crush and consume your confidence in who you are and *Whose* you are because he loves nothing more than to watch your decomposition and decay as his venomous darts filled with toxins lacerate and bruise, leaving you in the ashes and cinders. The enemy's trigger-happy mindset will try to trigger reactions deep within you because he wants to snuff out any ember of hope or optimism you have about your future. He can't afford any fragments of ash that have the potential to rekindle the fire of your faith in the knowledge that God rescues, redeems, and restores regardless of situations, otherwise those cinders could ignite something within you that will cause you to rise up and discover the warrior within.

Strongholds

Before we embark on our journey together, it's important to understand that the enemy will counteract your rising by attempting to erect strongholds in your mind. Never underestimate the enemy you're facing because he is as calculating as he is cunning. He has always been an opportunist who will find the tiniest chink in your armour to break down the trust you have in who God says He is and His promises. I have no doubt the enemy has certainly been rattled by your blood trail drying up because your wounds don't bleed out anymore now, they have turned into victorious scars. However, let's not get too sloppy or complacent in our approach because this is where the enemy can use strongholds to hinder the progress of your journey toward your transition and transformation, stopping you from rising up. And this is why it's so critical to be aware of the grip strongholds can have on our thinking. On that summer's morning when I heard God unmistakably say, *'Who chose you?'* it was a clear sign that my faulty thought pattern was going in the wrong direction. If there is one thing I have learned since that morning it's this—to reignite the fire within you're going to need the momentum of advancement in the right direction so you can shift from worrier to warrior by not allowing the strongholds to take hold of your thinking which can hold you back, delaying your progress in rising.

So, what are strongholds? Well, strongholds can be formed in our minds when false ideas, flimsy conclusions, philosophical reasoning, arguments, speculations, and theories disregard and reject God's authority.[3] The apostle Paul addresses the issue of strongholds and what weapons we must use to destroy them in 2 Corinthians 10:3-6. 'For although we live in the natural realm, we don't wage a military campaign employing human weapons, using manipulation to achieve our aims. Instead, our spiritual weapons are energized with divine power to effectively dismantle the defences behind which people hide. We can demolish every deceptive fantasy that opposes God and break through every arrogant attitude that is raised up in defiance of the true knowledge of God. We capture, like prisoners of war, every thought and insist that it bow in obedience to the Anointed One. Since we are armed with such dynamic weaponry, we stand ready to punish any trace of rebellion, as soon as you choose complete obedience.'[4] When Paul wrote his letter to the church in Corinth in second Corinthians, he was mindful that they had been heavily influenced by Hellenistic philosophy because philosophical reasoning, arguments and speculations were part of the culture. So, Paul was reminding the church in Corinth that they were not using human weapons but spiritual weapons that are not activated by presumptuous mindsets but by divine, otherworldly power. As Paul pointed out, this is dynamic weaponry! Synonyms for the word, dynamic are aggressive, changing, effective, forceful, influential, charismatic, and compelling.[5] Wow! That's some heavenly firepower right there!

The scars that tell your story are precisely why you need to protect them because the enemy gets the best of us on our worst days, and before we know what's hit us, we're looking around the forest floor for leaves to conceal and camouflage the shame we are feeling because we've allowed the enemy to hoodwink us again. But our weapons have enough gunpowder packed in each bullet to keep some distance between ourselves and the enemy, so we are able to gain the strength that gives us the momentum to rise up from the ashes. All the same, we have to keep firing our follow-up shots otherwise the enemy will have time to regroup his troops.

We Tell a Different Story

Just know that the enemy isn't one to take a follow-up shot on the chin and slither back into the pit where he came from. He's had plenty of practice in the act of warfare spanning over thousands of years and he is more than capable to execute his finely tuned strategies with pinpoint precision. Ever since Eve conversed with the serpent in the Garden, he's been very good at getting us to latch onto false ideas and flimsy conclusions that suggest God is holding out on us, so we doubt and question His authority. Don't get me wrong, in our modern, sophisticated, tech savvy world we can gain a better understanding of our humanity and why we think the way we do, but God never chose you or me because of our great wisdom. As Paul reminds us in 1 Corinthians 1:20-23, if we want to rise into the warriors God called us to be then our lives need to tell a different story. 'Hasn't God made fools out of those who count on the wisdom of this rebellious, broken world? For in God's deep wisdom, He made it so that the world could not even begin to comprehend Him through its own style of wisdom; in fact, God took immense pleasure in rescuing people of faith through the foolishness of the message we preach. It seems that Jews are always asking for signs and the Greeks are always on the prowl for wisdom. *But we tell a different story.*'[6] To break the power of strongholds our lives need to tell a different story to the one the world is narrating to us.

Of course, the enemy will happily fan the flames in our thinking when we start blaming someone else for our error, stirring an uprising within us rather than a rising up as blaming helps us to feel so much better because blame causes us to believe we're off the hook without sensing that we need to take any responsibly for our behaviour at bringing every thought that runs through our minds captive. St Teresa of Avila was onto something when she said, 'I know that strength arising from obedience has a way of simplifying things which seem impossible'. And just like that, this transparent, uncomplicated sixteenth-century Spanish nun, points us to a simple sign that is shaped into an arrow that points the way we need to take on this journey. An arrow that isn't dipped in an arrogant attitude that chooses to rise in defiance against God's authority and wisdom creating strongholds in our minds, it's an arrow that simply says, 'Obedience Is The Way'.

Simple, right?

But instead of following The Way, we run, because running is in our DNA. Sure, we've stopped running because our blood trail has dried up, wounds have turned into scars. But we can't stop running our mouths. Complaints just roll off our tongues in waves when we find ourselves out of our comfort zone and smack bang in the middle of the dusty desert plains because living in total obedience, the obedience that offers strength to do what God has asked us to do is just... well... too darn hard. But it's in the crucible of the desert where the transition of our transforming takes place. The desert is the place that causes change within you as you start to hunger for God's Word, you thirst for His direction, and you become desperate for His presence. Obedience that ignites a fire within no shifting sands can suffocate.

Let's Talk About Dogs

I know you're super keen to get started on our journey of reigniting the warrior within. You're ready for action, and I've talked long enough already. But there is one more thing I need to highlight before we head off with the prophetess, Miriam and make our way toward the edge of the forest if that's okay.

I want to talk about dogs.

Yes, I understand, this book draws parallels from the Phoenix, a mythical bird that dies in the combustion of flames and is reborn from the ashes, however, I wanted to talk about the power of a dog. An underdog to be more precise. We all love a good underdog story, right? We root for the one who is deemed as a poor, pathetic fool, the one who has been disregarded and overlooked but somehow proves to themselves and to everyone else that they are able to rise up against all odds. However, there is usually a character in the story who sees the underdog's potential and does whatever it takes to sabotage their efforts.[7] In the David verses Goliath theme, there's always a Saul who needs to stop the threat of the underdog taking over and make sure they are unable to fully transform and transition into their rising.

And this is where we circle back to the strongholds that create false ideas and conclusions in your mind reminding you over and over that you are never going to rise up and become a warrior instead of a worrier. Come on, seriously, why would God ever *choose* you? Let me warn you, dear friend, if you decide to listen to the enemy's snipes and sneers, if you allow these strongholds to smother your potential then it's in the ashes you'll stay. I know that's a little harsh, but the enemy will keep firing his ammunition, telling you that you're a poor, pathetic nobody and you should just get used to being disregarded, overlooked, undervalued and unnoticed by others because you'll never rise up into a somebody. If you keep believing those lies, then you may as well close this book right now and do something better to fill your time. But if what I've said resonates within you then don't waste another second, my friend! Get your walking boots on because we've got a long journey ahead of us. Remember, Satan is the character in your underdog story who sees your potential when nobody else does and he'll do anything to smother it. You need to know that although your potential may be buried, concealed, and covered in ashes at the moment, he *sees* it, and he's doing his best to sabotage your ability to believe that you have the courage to rise up.

And another thing before we get going.

Do you know why God chose you?

Don't worry about the answer because the apostle Paul can help you out here. 'For you see your calling, brethren, that not many wise according to the flesh, not many mighty, not many noble, are called. But God has chosen the foolish things of the world to put to shame the wise, and God has chosen the weak things of the world to put to shame the things which are mighty; and the base things of the world and the things which are despised God has chosen, and the things which are not, to bring to nothing the things that are, that no flesh should glory in His presence. But of Him you are in Christ Jesus, who became for us wisdom from God—and righteousness and sanctification and redemption—that, as it is written, He who glories, let him glory in the Lord.'[7] (1 Corinthians 1:26-31)

Foolish, weak, despised. Believe it or not, these are the qualities why God chose you. Seriously.

Because as Paul states, it's Christ's righteousness, sanctification and redemption that helps us to rise and nothing we do in helping ourselves to fan the flames will last, it can only be the power of God that will transform you so you can rise from the ashes and become the warrior you were always meant to be. This isn't another self-help book that offers the promise of a man-made victory, it is a guide, a challenge to help you realise the weapons you have been given is because you are fighting *from* the victory that's already been won! As Stanley Grenz and Jay Smith conclude, 'Within ourselves we have no answer. If there is a solution, it must come from beyond ourselves.'[8] And this is why this follow-up shot is so important. God *must* be the One who leads you through your transition and transformation. It's His transforming power that causes you to rise and rekindle the warrior within you, otherwise you'll be right back where I first found you, running and hiding because of the blood trail following behind you.

Well, my friend, I think you're set. I think it's finally time we got moving. So, tighten up those bootlaces and let's embark on a journey that will not only transform you but reignite the warrior within.

Endnotes: Chapter One

Ref 1   Quote by Teresa of Avila, *Interior Castle*. Website: goodreads.com

Ref 2   John 15:16. *Amplified Holy Compact Bible: Captures the Full Meaning behind the Original Greek and Hebrew*. 2015. Grand Rapids, Michigan: Zondervan.

Ref 3   Simmons, Brian. 2018. *The Passion Translation New Testament (2nd Edition)*. Broadstreet Publishing Group LLC. (Bible commentary)

Ref 4   2 Corinthians 10:3-6. Simmons, Brian. 2018. *The Passion Translation New Testament (2nd Edition)*. Broadstreet Publishing Group LLC.

Ref 5   Website: thesaurus.com

Ref 6   1 Corinthians 1:20-23. Ecclesia Bible Society. 2012. *The Voice Bible: Step into the Story of Scripture*. Nashville: Thomas Nelson

Ref 7   Brody, Jessica. 2018. *Save The Cat! Writes A Novel: The Last Book on Novel Writing You'll Ever Need*' California: Ten Speed Press.

Ref 8   1 Corinthians 1:26-31. *Spiritual Warfare Bible*. 2012. Lake Mary, Florida, Charisma House.

Ref 9   Grenz, Stanley J, and Jay T. Smith. 2015. *Created For Community : Connecting Christian Belief with Christian Living*. Grand Rapids, Mi: Baker Academic.

CHAPTER TWO

The Firebird

*'Then I said, "I shall die in my nest,
and multiply my days as the sand."'*[1]
JOB 29:18

The Phoenix. A magnificent, brightly coloured bird that symbolises renewal and rebirth found in Greek and Egyptian mythologies because of its ability to rise up out of its own ashes. According to Egyptian mythology, this legendary bird so captivated the sun god Apollo's attention by its melodic dawn song, he not only stopped his chariot to listen to the Phoenix singing but he also stopped the sun too.[2] In Greek mythology, the Phoenix was believed to have lived for 500 years before it was consumed by fire and then resurrected three days later from the ashes. The meaning of the word, 'Phoenix' in ancient Greek is 'dark red' because its bright and colourful plumage is a symbol of hope and optimism, of better things to come.[3] This fascinating firebird has certainly held interest and attention over the centuries because it symbolises a person's comeback when everything seems lost, and if ever there was someone who could talk to us about comebacks, it's Job. We find him using the metaphor of the Phoenix when he's feeling content and joyful even though he continues to go through his trials. 'Then I said, "I shall die in my nest, and multiply my days as the sand".' (Job 29:18) One translation replaces the word 'sand' with the word 'phoenix'.[4] Job goes on, 'My root is spread out to the waters, and the dew lies all night on my branch. My glory is fresh within me, and my bow is renewed in my hand.'[5] According to biblical commentary the bow being renewed was Job feeling born new, hence the Phoenix reference. It meant that he hadn't felt like an overused bow that had turned dry or brittle, losing its power because it had been compressed, bent, or stretched.[6] Job's life had certainly turned to ashes, but he wasn't feeling arid or bare, he was sensing a comeback, a resurrection, a rising.

The journey to becoming an effective warrior means you're going to have to allow for some compressing, you're going to have to be a little bent out of shape and most definitely you will be stretched along the path to rising. Job teaches us that God will never abandon us even in the fiery trials because those are the moments where the warrior is born anew. And yet, we are reluctant to go through the process of becoming a warrior as indecisive hesitation floods our souls when the thought of fire and ashes overshadows our desire to become transformed. It is these doubts and worries that stop us from facing the crucible that will reignite the warrior within. For the Phoenix to rise, for the rebirth to happen and the physical process of the flames to consume everything old, the firebird must make a choice to trust, and if it does, then the all-consuming fire will shed the old self and bring forth the new. Like the Phoenix, you must allow yourself to become totally abandoned to the process, giving God permission to let His fierce fire of correction burn everything that is shakeable within your faith leaving only what is unshakeable. The fire's purpose is not to destroy but rather it's a necessity that prepares you to rise up and become who you were called to be.

An Awkward Appearance

What we all need to know is, what's the time frame of the Phoenix being consumed by the fire and flames before its reduced down to a pile of ashes? How long does it watch all its majestic, beautiful feathers catch alight that make up its dark red plumage before it finds the strength to rise? Is there a part of the process where it looks more like a half plucked barbequed chicken in the flames until it's rebirthed anew? I mean, sure, everybody loves the metaphor of the Phoenix, they appreciate how this majestic firebird rises from the ashes, triumphant and born anew, but if we're honest with ourselves, we don't really like the slow burn of what can sometimes become a painful journey of changes because secretly we want the quick fix, we want the warrior part pronto. ASAP. We don't want to appear like a blundering, half-plucked bird whose bulky, bumbling moments reveal we're needing to go through something. However, God is in the business of rescue and redemption, not a slight improvement here and there. As C.S. Lewis points out, 'It is not like teaching a horse to jump better and better but like turning a horse into a winged creature... once it has got its wings, it will soar over fences... but there may be a period, while the wings are just beginning to grow, when it cannot do so: and at that stage the lumps on the shoulders... may give an awkward appearance."[7] We'd rather not go through the awkwardness of looking incompetent and inexperienced but the irony is that we can only become the warrior if we allow God to do some bending, compressing, and stretching on the inside of us. Those majestic dark red wings of yours will possibly be charred into mere stumps throughout this journey that take on an awkward appearance through the flames, but if you are willing to grow and change, I believe that's where true, lasting transformation takes place. Remember the scrawny shepherd boy David? He looked nothing like the brave warrior who would take Saul's place as the next king of Israel because 'people judge by outward appearance, but the Lord looks at the heart' as it states in 1 Samuel 16:7. (NLT) The world will tell us what a warrior *should* look like, however, what a true warrior actually *does* look like is very different from God's point of view. The one who's heart is willing to take the inner journey of discovering who they truly are is the one who is able to find the strength and courage to rise up.

Here I Am, Send Me!

If there is one thing our fearless leader, Miriam will not stand for its blended ideas that can lead us down the wrong path. The danger of getting too carried away with Egyptian and Greek mythologies of the Phoenix is that this firebird's melodic dawn song can become so hypnotic that we'll end up be lulled into a slumber that will only produce inactivity. This sluggish behaviour is what our enemy wants because our follow-up shot cannot be fired if we find ourselves in a comatose state. Miriam understands all too well the heartache of taking on myths and mindsets that set themselves up against the authority of God. The Egyptians were the embodiment of this behaviour and the Israelites had become so ingrained in the culture over the years that it took another forty long, gruelling years in the wilderness to shake it off. As Richard Ritenbaugh warns, 'God needs us on the same page as Him. And if it means turning our lives upside down, turning us inside out, He'll do it, because He loves us.' [8] Miriam is an expert at watching God turn your life inside out and upside down because of how much He loves us, and He'll bring His cleansing fire to do it. The fire that burns up the dross of old mindsets, getting rid of deep-set theories that cling to our thinking.

Even the prophet Isaiah needed cleansing so his life could be redirected. 'Then one of the flaming creatures flew to me holding a red-hot ember which it had taken from God's table, the temple altar, with a pair of tongs. The creature held it to my lips. Look! With the touch of this burning ember on your lips, your guilt is turned away; all your faults and wrongdoings are forgiven. Then I heard the Lord's voice. Whom shall I send? Who will go for Us? Here I am! Send me."[9] Isaiah's response when he realised he was seeing a vision of God sitting on a throne and His royal robe filled the temple, the prophet became alert to his condition and this awareness filled him with a deep desire to be changed from the inside out so he was ready for God to use him.

No Power Over You Anymore

So, you must be wondering what this follow-shot is and perhaps you've never met our daring, bold leader and prophetess,

Miriam, in between the pages of the story of the Exodus. Miriam is possibly best known for her lively impromptu tambourine song and dance routine to God after He delivered the Israelites out of Egypt. With power-packed lyrics in her song like 'Sing to the Lord, for He has triumphed gloriously and is highly exalted; the horse and rider He has hurled into the sea'[10] becoming the moment Miriam influenced other women to follow her in praising and thanking God because He safely rescued them from their enemy, Pharaoh, by creating a path through the Red Sea, means your follow-up shot will do the same. A powerful weapon against the enemy, a victory song you'll compose and sing, celebrating that God is a Rescuer and a Deliverer, reminding the enemy he has no power over you anymore.

Ever listened to a song and within seconds old memories start flooding into your mind? It's the same reason they formulated songs in ancient times. Of course, they never had recording devices back then, so they wrote victory songs to record the moment the battle was won over their enemies.[11] This is why Deborah's song is mentioned in the book of Judges as she arose to be the mother to Israel. 'Sing this song... all of you who now hear the sound of shepherds at the watering places, proclaim the just victories of the Eternal, the just triumphs of His destitute people in Israel... wake up, wake up Deborah! Wake up, wake up and sing!'[12] It's time to wake up and sing, dear friend, and let the fire of God rebirth the warrior within because the enemy will keep you going around in circles in that comfort zone until you become dizzy! If you're feeling that internal agitation, that tension that is calling you to take the next courageous step that's good because it means your warrior is needing to be awakened. Yes, it may possibly get a little painful and perhaps the road may be rough in some parts of the journey that could cause you to give up and give in, but this is where the melody is formed, this is where the victory lyrics are developed. As theologian, pastor, and writer Dr. A.W. Tozer once said, 'This is why I do not like the kind of evangelism that sugar-coats everything. I believe there ought to be a cry of pain. I think there ought to be a birth from within.'[13] At its core, birthing is a procedure to deliver children. It's a pain from within that delivers something. A plan that causes you to step up and lean in wholeheartedly because giving birth isn't about you anymore, it's about another human that needs to be delivered. And as Tozer suggests, the sickly-sweet coating some spread over the Christian way of life makes it more pleasant and acceptable that it really is. Don't get me wrong, God blesses, He favours, He loves but like a good Father, He has a plan, a procedure to deliver people out from the under the oppression of the enemy that could involve some pain.

So, let's get to know Miriam a little better, shall we? Let's rewind her journey right to the start of when the warrior within her was ignited. Long before her brother was commissioned in the desert to deliver God's people out of Egypt because God had heard their deep cry of suffering and pain. Moses' life could have been very short-lived, however, thanks to two courageous warriors who had decided that they were not going to follow a plan, a procedure that made sure baby boys were not going to be delivered, they assisted a woman who was in the throes of labour pains and helped to deliver a baby boy, who unbeknown to them, would one day become a deliverer himself.

Endnotes: Chapter Two

Ref 1 Job 29:18. *Spiritual Warfare Bible.* 2012. Lake Mary, Florida, Charisma House.

Ref 2 Website: mocomi.com/what-is-phoenix/

Ref 3 Website: biblekeeper.com/ phoenix meaning 'dark red'

Ref 4 Website: biblestudytools.com/job/29-18-compare.html

Ref 5 Job 29:18-20. *Spiritual Warfare Bible.* 2012. Lake Mary, Florida, Charisma House.

Ref 6 Walton, John H, Victor Harold Matthews, and Mark William Chavalas. 2000.*The IVP Bible Background Commentary Old Testament.* Downers Grove, Ill. Intervarsity Press.

Ref 7 Lewis, C.S. 2017. *Mere Christianity.* Harpercollins Publishers. (Orig. pub. 1952)

Ref 8 Ritenbaugh, Richard T. "How to Survive Exile" Sermon. Website: bibletools.org.

Ref 9 Isaiah 6:6-8 Ecclesia Bible Society. 2012. *The Voice Bible: Step into the Story of Scripture.* Nashville: Thomas Nelson

Ref 10 Exodus 15:21. *Amplified Holy Compact Bible: Captures the Full Meaning behind the Original Greek and Hebrew.* 2015. Grand Rapids, Michigan: Zondervan.

Ref 11 Walton, John H, Victor Harold Matthews, and Mark William Chavalas. 2000.*The IVP Bible Background Commentary Old Testament.* Downers Grove, Ill. Intervarsity Press.

Ref 12 Judges 5:10-12. Ecclesia Bible Society. 2012. *The Voice Bible: Step into the Story of Scripture.* Nashville: Thomas Nelson

Ref 13 Tozer, A.W., and James L. Snyder 2020. *The Fire of God's Presence: Drawing near to a Holy God.* Grand Rapids: Bethany House Publishers.

CHAPTER THREE

Two Stones

'Your greatest acts of courage are the moments you forget about yourself, and you only think about others.' [1]
ERWIN MCMANUS

What thoughts come to mind when you think about what makes a leader? Perhaps they are a risk taker, a visionary, they value authenticity and integrity, they display confidence when needed, they make a difference in the lives of others, or is it their vulnerability in sharing their weaknesses? All these things can help make a leader into a great leader, however, the one trait of a leader that can sometimes get overlooked is courage. Courage is when someone decides to take action and speak up about something that goes against their convictions, regardless of the consequences of their own well-being. One of the character traits of a warrior is courage and it's developed from within as they face conflict and challenges head on rather than avoid them. In most stories about warriors, 'The major prop is a weapon of some kind'[2] according to Carol S.

Pearson Ph.D. that helps the warrior win the day, and it's in the tight moments the weapon of courage is wielded by the warrior because keeping quiet isn't an option anymore. Courage doesn't come in the absence of fear but through the controlling and harnessing of the fear we're feeling as we choose to do the right thing regardless of the threats of possible dangers or uncertainties. Sometimes the warrior has no time to write out a courageous step-by-step plan before showing an act of bravery and courage, they just choose, in the moment, to do something about an injustice no matter how hard it feels.[3]

Beautifully Splendid

In Exodus 1:17 we find two courageous midwives whose names were Shiphrah and Puah. The name Shiphrah means 'splendid', and the name Puah means 'beautiful',[4] and these women showed a warrior's heart so beautifully and so splendidly through a terrible situation they found themselves in when they chose to bravely defy a royal decree. The edict to throw all male babies into the Nile River moments after their delivery had come straight from the Pharaoh himself. To understand the sheer weight backing up this decree, Pharaohs who ruled over Egypt were not treated as mere men who just set laws and demanded order over the land. No, they were considered a god, an embodiment, and an advocate of the Egyptian god, Horus.[5] However, as with all human monarchs, whether they are perceived as a god or not, Pharaohs do eventually die, and a new ruler takes their place. Unfortunately, the new Pharaoh in this story was as nasty as he was ignorant to Egypt's history as he had never heard of Joseph and his story of how he went from prisoner to Prime Minister over Egypt because he had a God-given gift of interpreting dreams. This reigning ruler was only interested in the servitude labour force the Israelite people represented and their unquestionable obedience to his will rather than all that touchy-feely stuff the other weak Pharaoh had expressed to God's chosen people in the past. This paranoid Pharaoh became unreasonably suspicious of the growing number of Israelites and was extremely bothered about them. His concern was that if they kept growing in numbers, they would eventually outnumber the Egyptians which could start an uprising as the Israelites may decide to join the enemy nations and, eventually, they could turn on Egypt. So, to prevent this from happening Pharaoh hatched a perverted plan that needed the help of the ones who delivered the babies.

'Then the king of Egypt spoke to the Hebrew midwives, of whom the name of one was Shiphrah and the name of the other Puah; and he said, "When you do the duties of a midwife for the Hebrew women, and see them on the birthstools, if it is a son, then you shall kill him; but if it is a daughter, then she shall live."'[6] To disobey this order would most likely end in execution, so the midwives own views and values would have possibly had to have been hidden and supressed as they listened to Pharaoh's diabolical decree. The two midwives, Shiphrah and Puah, may have glanced at each other as they left the royal court in a way that only two allies who had decided to make a pact between each other would do. What would they decide as they were now confronted with a situation that breached their core values? Were they going to shrink back and allow fear to rule them and only think about themselves or were they going to go against Pharaoh and push through the fears that surrounded their souls for the sake of saving others? The options were as hard as they were narrow because not only the physical safety of the male babies they were delivering was in jeopardy but their own physical safety if word got back to Pharaoh that they chose to willingly disobey his decree. We need to understand, becoming a warrior isn't about sword fights and chivalry, fighting off dragons and winning over princess's hearts, it's about forgetting about yourself and thinking of others. As the Native American, Sitting Bull, Hunkpapa Lakota Sioux so rightly stated, 'The warrior, for us, is one who sacrifices himself for the good of others. His task is to take care of the elderly, the defenceless, those who cannot provide for themselves, and above all, the children—the future of humanity.'[7] These two midwives feared someone much bigger and far more powerful than Pharaoh—they feared God. 'But the midwives feared God and did not do as the king of Egypt commanded them but saved the male children alive.'[8] I need you to know something, dear friend, fearing something will stop you from rising but fearing God will help you to find the courage to rise. Many believers struggle with what the term 'fearing God' means because they think it's a fear that fills you with anxiety and dread. But the fear of God is a Holy reverence to who God is and what He is capable of. It is to esteem and be in adoration of His majesty and deity, someone who is worthy of all our praise and worship. I want to spend a little time on the fear of God and how it helps the warrior to rise up, but I sense the wisdom of Miriam and what she has to offer in this area of fearing the Lord will benefit you more if we are a little further and deeper into our journey to have that weighty discussion, so I'll save that thought for another chapter.

Not Just a Baby Was Birthed That Day

Possibly there were far more midwives to deliver Hebrew babies than Shiphrah and Puah in the regions that made up Egypt, but these two women are prominent in the story at the start of the book of Exodus because they feared God more than they feared Pharaoh which says a lot about their character. They probably directed the other midwives who were under their charge to not drown the male babies in the Nile River as Pharaoh had decreed. Good news for the home of Amram, because his wife, Jochebed, was in the ache, discomfort, and pangs of labour. Midwives played an important role in the whole process of pregnancy as this role may have been given to women who were unable to have children of their own, thus freeing them to help deliver babies. However, the Bible does not state that a designated midwife was with Jochebed when she delivered her baby boy. Nevertheless, ancient Near Eastern deliveries of babies involved all the female family members to help the mother with the birth of the baby.[9] With this knowledge it was highly possible Miriam was present when her baby brother was born. To assist with the birth, the women used gravity to aid the mother while she delivered her baby. This meant the mother either placed her feet or kneeled on birthing bricks to position herself for the birth and this elevation of the mother helped give the midwife more room to do her work.[9] The delivery stool which literally means 'two stones' [10] were the support the mother needed in the imminent arrival of their baby. As I mentioned earlier, the name Shiphrah means 'splendid', and the name Puah means 'beautiful', and although these two women were possibly not the midwives who were with Jochebed when she delivered their future deliverer, they were the two supporting stones that helped to deliver male babies, making sure they were not drowned in the Nile River.

These two warriors bravely chose to go against the royal decree and this knowledge possibly birthed something on the inside of the young girl named Miriam, who perhaps helped these women as they assisted the other women in birth. Miriam could have felt something splendid, something beautiful from the spark of knowing these midwives bravely rose in the face of adversity and it was their courage that kindled the tinder surrounding her tender young heart. As she watched her mother boldly give birth to a child she knew would one day do something special, she may have been thinking about the two courageous midwives who chose to disobey a royal decree. Three women whose actions helped Miriam understand that true warriors forget about themselves and think about others when it came time to do the right thing. With the unmoveable character traits of his mother and two courageous women, Moses was spared from the cruel fate that Pharaoh demanded all midwives take part in. The delivery stool played an important part in helping to deliver a deliverer, it supported the mother as she went through the painful process of each stage in the birth. Not only that, but splendid Shiphrah and beautiful Puah supported Jochebed in her time of need, even if it was possibly from afar.

Three courageous warrior women, Shiphrah, Puah, and Jochebed, supported each other through the difficulty and messiness of birthing something were like a three-strand cord that could not be easily broken.[11] Women who supported other women regardless of Pharaoh's ridiculous rule and the consequences they could face because of their courage. And as we learn to rise up into our destiny, we need the support, strength, and courage of strong characters, like the midwives and Moses' mother, who can bear the weight of responsibility by helping us through the early crucial stages of rising up.

Can You Hear It?

Looking back on my own journey of leadership, I think about the many warrior women who have supported me over the years. As I watched, admired, and observed these fearless, brave women, some from afar and a select few who gladly chose to become my mentors, the ones who could bear the weight of responsibility by taking care of me while I developed my wings in leadership, in my writing, and in my calling were with me during those early crucial stages of becoming the leader I am today. Over time as I observed these women, I became mindful of how many times they forgot about themselves and chose to serve others regardless of their own difficult circumstances. Perhaps there were times when my women friends often wondered to themselves if they had what it takes to support someone who was in the early messy stages of birthing a dream they felt God had developed on the inside of them. However, I believe, the warrior within them didn't need to know whether they had what it takes to support me, it didn't matter, because they just gave what needed to be given, and God provided it to them time and time again. They displayed to me their courage and the strength of their character in the day-to-day, unapplauded, unappreciated moments, and I realised that those were the moments where true warriors are shaped and formed. Like Shiphrah and Puah, developing their reputations was not as important to them as developing their character and although the Hebrews were despised, oppressed and were in slavery they *still* flourished. 'But the harder the slave drivers pushed the Israelites, the more rapidly they had children and spread throughout the land.'[12] A song rose up regardless of the obstacles the enemy put in the Israelites way and Pharaoh had tuned into the sound of this weapon. 'When Egypt's king heard this news, he sent for the midwives. "Why have you disobeyed my orders and allowed the boys to live?"' I so admire Shiphrah and Puah's response because it was so well thought out, so calmly and cleverly executed that Pharaoh accepted their report. "Because unlike Egyptian women, Hebrew women are hearty and energetic, and they give birth before the midwife arrives to help."[13] Can you hear it? The song these two women sang. The follow-up shot that was aimed straight at the Pharaoh's selfish plan came at him in stereo. Pharaoh's motive behind his decree of drowning male babies was more about his reputation as a leader. He was more concerned with looking good rather than working on his character, and these two women made it very clear that their character was far more important to them than their reputation. Tim Hawkins puts it another way, 'Your character is what you're really like on the inside whether anyone knows about it or not... if you have a good character—a Christ-like character—an honest character—then no one can ever take that away from you.'[14] I know what you're thinking, the midwives lied to Pharaoh. I'll admit this isn't a great character trait for a warrior. However, think about the situation they were in for a minute. Many lives were on the line, including Moses'. These midwives' motive behind their lie was for selfless reasons not selfish ones. For all they knew they could have possibly still been executed for disobeying Pharaoh's decree regardless of their answer. But God looked after them 'Because the midwives respected God, He blessed them with families of their own.'[15]

Miriam perhaps heard the story about the two courageous midwives taking a stand before Pharaoh to save many others. Maybe they were the subject of conversation at the watering wells where the women gathered? We shall never know. But one thing is clear, Miriam witnessed women supporting other women when she was just a young girl, and she caught the sound of their robust courage. The song that arose from the chorus of a three-strand cord which was made up of her mother and the two midwives and how their follow-up shot stopped an enemy in his tracks. A weapon of selfless bravery that was wielded by two splendid, beautiful warriors who chose character over reputation because they decided to forget about themselves and help others instead.

Endnotes: Chapter Three

Ref 1   'Rise to your legend' YouTube watch sermon. Erwin McManus

Ref 2   Pearson, Carol S. Ph.D. The Hero Within. 'Are You A Warrior? And if so, What Kind?' April 23, 2018. Website: psychologytoday.com

Ref 3   Laurie, Greg. Website: crosswalk.com/faith/spiritual-life/what-does-it-look-like-to-have-true-courage. Harvest Christian Fellowship. 31st March 2020.

Ref 4   Kohlmeyer, Denise. '3 Reasons you should know the courageous story of Shiprah and Puah'. Website: crosswalk.com.

Ref 5   Pfeiffer, Charles F. 1973. Old Testament History. Grand Rapids, Mich.: Baker Book House, (Printing.

Ref 6   Exodus 1:15-16. *Spiritual Warfare Bible. 2012. Lake Mary, Florida, Charisma House.*

Ref 7   pbs.org. What does it mean to be a warrior? The Warrior Tradition.

Ref 8   Exodus 1: 17 *Spiritual Warfare Bible. 2012. Lake Mary, Florida, Charisma House.*

Ref 9   Rathkamp, Quinn, "Childbirth Through Time" (2017) . *WWU Honors Program Senior Projects.* 56. Western Washington University. Website: cedar.wwu.edu.

Ref 10   Bible commentary. Syswerda, Jean, and Faith Organization.2001. NIV Women of Faith Study Bible: New International Version. Grand Rapids, Mich.: Zondervan.

Ref 11   Ecclesiastes 4:12. Ecclesia Bible Society. 2012. *The Voice Bible: Step into the Story of Scripture.* Nashville: Thomas Nelson

Ref 12   Exodus 1:12 Ecclesia Bible Society. 2012. *The Voice Bible: Step into the Story of Scripture.* Nashville: Thomas Nelson

Ref 13   Exodus 1:18-19 Ecclesia Bible Society. 2012. *The Voice Bible: Step into the Story of Scripture.* Nashville: Thomas Nelson

Ref 14   Hawkins, Tim. *The Heart of Leadership: The three building blocks for every leader.* Leaders Unlimited. 2022.

Ref 15   Exodus 1:20 Ecclesia Bible Society. 2012. *The Voice Bible: Step into the Story of Scripture.* Nashville: Thomas Nelson

CHAPTER FOUR

I Say to You, Get Up!

*'We don't screw up by saying yes to the wrong things;
we screw up by letting all the floats in the parade pass us by
and never jumping on one of them for a ride to the end.'* [1]
ANNIE F. DOWNS

If you've navigated a few decades of life and have the skinned knees and scars to prove it, you've most likely had a conversation with yourself at some point about what would be the one piece of advice you would give to your younger self. I'm sure you have a good deal of suggestions that you would bombard your younger self with and some time-learned observations that could do with a few tweaks here and there. However, if we're going to be yammering on at our younger selves, we need to keep one thing in mind. We are a child and our attention span when some kind, older person is giving us some good 'advice' would be very, and I mean very, limited. Now, I'm speaking from my own experience, perhaps you were a better listener when you were growing up than myself, which possibly did you a great service in not landing in as much trouble as I did. However, my point is that I want you to put yourself back into those black, laced up childhood shoes of yours. You know, the ones your mother made you wear because they were far more sensible than the sparkly, heeled ones you really wanted in the shoe shop. I want you, just for a moment, to consider if you would remember or even care about the long list of instructions you were going to blast your younger self with so that your future would turn out perfect.

I thought not.

What usually works with children is one sentence that encapsulates everything you want to say and making that the most important thing that needs to be said. Not so easy to achieve, right? The thing is, I believe our younger self really doesn't need to hear a ten-paged essay on how to conquer life's ups and downs, just one sentence that pinpoints the biggest challenge we have struggled with throughout our lives would suffice. How about you, dear friend, what would be the one sentence you'd tell your younger self? Mine would be 'Stop hiding who you are when others feel insecure around you' which would have the knock-on effect of stopping me from underestimating and downplaying my God-given talents. It would help me from self-sabotaging things when it all becomes way too uncomfortable and too scary. It would teach me to be kinder to myself when I make mistakes and to give myself more grace when I mess things up, and finally, that one sentence would keep me staying in the moments when being seen for who I truly am would have been far better than running away and hiding. See how that one sentence stopped the flow of all my other issues? I wonder what the one sentence our daring, courageous leader, Miriam would tell her younger self?

A Different Plan

In the last chapter we observed a young Miriam listening to the sound of courage as two warriors wielded their follow-up shot against a paranoid Pharaoh who couldn't stop a song rising up in the face of his diabolical plan. Now we find Miriam once again, stoking the fires that were kindled inside of her as she follows the instructions of another plan. Except this plan was to make sure that a deliverer was delivered into the right hands and not submerged under the waters of the Nile. Scholars have different opinions on the age gap between Miriam and Moses. Some sources suggest a seven-year gap while others propose that Miriam was much older. But regardless of the age difference, Miriam, according to tradition, was a prophetess even in her younger years, for she prophesied that her sibling would be the one to bring redemption to God's chosen people.[2] And for this reason she knew her role in God's plan was to help her baby brother survive Pharaoh's insane intention to kill all male babies. Yes, that's right, even after Shiphrah and Puah's courageous attempt at slowing down the royal decree, Pharaoh commands his people by saying, 'Every son who is born you shall cast into the river, and every daughter you shall save alive.'[3] Clearly Pharaoh could no longer trust the midwives to execute his plan, so he made sure *all* his subjects did what he demanded.

Jochebed needed a different plan to keep her baby boy alive, so she hid him. 'When she saw that he was (especially) beautiful and healthy, she hid him for three months (to protect him from the Egyptians) When she could no longer hide him, she got him a basket (chest) made of papyrus reeds and covered it with tar and pitch (making it waterproof). Then she put the child in it and set it among the reeds by the bank of the Nile.'[4] I stand in appreciation of Jochebed. Not only did she keep her baby hidden from the Egyptians for three months, but she also knew that the inevitable day would come when she would have to give her son away if he was to have any chance of survival. Perhaps her prophetess daughter, Miriam, helped her mother come up with the plan? Regardless, Jochebed's plan mirrored the ancient stories of heroes being spared at birth where a royal dignitary who had been abandoned to fate was miraculously spared and then raised by common people.[5] The plan also reflected the ancient story of Noah following God's step-by-step plan to build an ark that would save each animal and deliver his family as he had to cover the ark 'inside and out with pitch.'[6] Jochebed had completed phase one of the plan by preparing the watertight vessel which was to carry her baby safely down the river. The next step required her daughter to play a courageous role in this different, God-breathed plan, for she knew everything depended on this moment and it was crucial that this part of the plan was done right. 'And his sister (Miriam) stood some distance away to find out what would happen to him.'[7]

I can see you're drawn into the backstory of our fearless leader, Miriam, and I can sense you need to ask her the question I asked you earlier as she recalls the pivotal moments that help turn her into a warrior. What you want to know while you're journeying with Miriam is what she would say to her younger self if she could go back in time. What would be the one sentence she would tell the girl hiding in the banks of the Nile, feeling the pressure to rise up. After a slight pause Miriam would probably look you straight in the eye and say, 'The one sentence I would tell my younger self is this—lean forward into God's promises and don't shrink back.'

Get a Handle on Your Weapon

I just want to pause for a moment before we continue on our warrior adventure because I need you to be aware of something that will possibly interest you. In ancient times the sticky substance Jochebed used to waterproof her baby's basket for its precarious journey down the Nile River was commonly known as bitumen and was used as a gluey adhesive to secure the handles on weapons.[8] Don't you just love this?! The basket that a future deliverer of God's people was placed in was surrounded by a component that was used to help a warrior handle their weapon.

Wow!

You see, this is where the enemy gets into the wounded warrior's thinking. Recall back to the moment Jesus touched your soul in that little wooden cabin in the forest as He slowly turned your wounds into victorious scars. He told you something that you need to now remember on this journey of rising. He said to you that 'the one who has been wounded in the battle has a deep dread of being abandoned.'[9] When you get a handle on your weapon and you understand the power behind the follow-up shot and how to handle it well, the enemy will hinder your progress and continually target your thoughts back to the moments in your past where you felt totally discarded and deserted. However, in your journey to reigniting the warrior within He is now closer to you than ever because He promised in John 14:16-18 that He has asked the Father, 'and He will give you another Helper (Comforter, Advocate, Intercessor—Counsellor,

Strengthener, Standby), to be with you forever—the Spirit of Truth, whom the world cannot receive (and take to its heart) because it does not see Him or know Him, but you know Him because He (the Holy Spirit) remains with you continually and will be in you. "I will not leave you as orphans (comfortless, bereaved, and helpless); I will come (back) to you."'[10]

Throughout this journey, there will be choices you'll have to make and transitions that will be difficult to work through as you emerge from the ashes and learn to rise up into the warrior you know you need to be. A song is rising within you dear friend and the follow-up shot is forming, but you're probably thinking about those pleasant, comfortable feelings that cause you to want to close your eyes just for a moment. Yes, settle down into those nice, warm ashes that have made you feel so safe and secure. Of course, no one is going to stop you because you always have a choice. Agreed? This could be the moment where your journey ends and no one is going to think bad of you for trying. No one will shame you because you gave it your best shot. Right?

Hmmm. Does all this sound familiar? Have your ears been listening to the enemy's lies instead of tuning into the sound of God's Truth? The help from the Comforter isn't to keep you comfortable. As Bill Johnson suggests, 'What do I trust most, my ability to be deceived or His ability to keep me?'[11] You can either downplay, shelve, self-sabotage and possibly even ignore the call to become a warrior and allow that passion to be snuffed out by the enemy's deception, or you can learn to understand how the follow-up shot is used to effectively stop the enemy from hunting you down over and over again.

It's totally up to you.

Because the truth is that we want to ignite the warrior within but 'we're still maddeningly hardwired to resist voluntarily making the very changes it often takes to get what we want' as Lisa Cron so boldly states.[12] It is so easy to look at Miriam's story when we have the panoramic view of the chain of events that made up her life. The smooth and straightforward path from our bird's eye view seems so effortless as we listen to her story and applaud her courage and determination to fulfill her dream of coming out of slavery and moving toward the Promised Land. Our fear of wondering if we will be wounded again and if we will face defeat outweighs the need of the warrior rising up. So, we run and we hide within the ashes where our dreams of making a difference cannot be poked or prodded because the battle that rages on the inside of us reminds us that we're not brave or courageous like Miriam, we are bereaved and helpless, so leave us be and let the warrior perish within the cinders. You believe your scars disqualify you, but I want you to know that those marks that you bear, the wounds that have become victorious scars they're not a sign of your weaknesses my friend, they are what give you the strength and courage to rise up. Listen to me dear warrior. You can't set the world on fire if you stay hidden, stay small and stay quiet, okay? Others need you to reignite the warrior within and the Comforter, Miriam, and myself will be right beside you, cheering you on.

Talitha Kum!

Why do we believe the lies from our enemy? The one who keeps constantly reminding us that what seems dead in our lives cannot be resurrected from the ashes? As we have already discussed about the one sentence we would tell our younger selves, as adults it is important for God to take us by the hand

and tell us one sentence that can speak life back into the child inside of us, so we are able to rise. He needs to resurrect the childlike faith we felt died within us as the wounds that bled out and the pain we bore caused a grief within us that lost little fragments of ourselves along the way. He needs to speak life back into our inner child, the one who never lost sight of His marvellous treasures because they stopped and saw the wonderment and beauty within the normal moments through their day-to-day lives. Seeing a beautiful butterfly fluttering from petal to petal in the garden, or finding a little, yellow leaf in the shape of a heart, shaped their childlike hearts into trusting the One who holds their tender, young at heart faith in the palm of His mighty hand. To become the warrior God calls us to be we need to awaken our childlike faith that once upon a time, long, long ago allowed God to take us by the hand and lead us into an adventure where we never once questioned His guidance. We just trusted and followed while He led and didn't worry about where we would end up.

In Mark chapter 5 we see the unfolding of a miracle. A moment where hope seems extinguished and grief carries its scars. Jairus, a synagogue official knew his daughter was dying and he falls at the feet of Jesus and begs Him for a miracle. I'll let you read the story for yourself...

'...some people came from the synagogue official's house, saying (to Jairus), "Your daughter has died; why bother the Teacher any longer?" Overhearing what was being said, Jesus said to the synagogue official, "Do not be afraid; only keep on believing (in Me and my power)." And He allowed no one to go with Him (as witnesses), except Peter and James and John the brother of James. They came to the house of the synagogue official; and He looked (with understanding) at the uproar and commotion, and people loudly weeping and wailing (in mourning). When He had gone in, He said to them, "Why make a commotion and weep? The child has not died but is sleeping." They began laughing (scornfully) at Him (because they knew the child was dead). But He made them all go outside and took along the child's father and mother and His own (three) companions and entered the room where the child was.

Taking the child's hand, He said (tenderly) to her, *"Talitha kum!"*—which translated (from Aramaic) means, "Little girl, I say to you, get up!" The little girl immediately got up and began to walk, for she was twelve years old. And immediately they (who witnessed the child's resurrection) were overcome with great wonder and utter amazement.'[13] God is telling you His one sentence to your younger self, 'Little girl, (or boy) I say to you, get up!'

Get up! Get up! GET UP!

The enemy wants you to keep listening to the sound of uproar, commotion, and mourning. He wants you to tune into the frequency of all the weeping and wailing of what once was. However, we have news for him because the sound of the follow-up shot is rising and Jesus is saying to you, 'Do not be afraid; only keep on believing (in Me and my power).' Jesus' resurrection power is going to resurrect your childlike faith and people will take one look at you and will be overcome with great wonder and utter amazement.

Are you prepared to make the changes that ignites the warrior within?

Then dust yourself down and let's get moving!

Endnotes: Chapter Four

Ref 1   Downs, Annie F. *'100 Days to Brave: Devotions for Unlocking Your Most Courageous Self'* Zondervan. 2017.

Ref 2   jewishvirtuallibrary.org/Miriam

Ref 3   Exodus 1:22 *Spiritual Warfare Bible*. 2012. Lake Mary, Florida, Charisma House.

Ref 4   Exodus 2:2-3 *Amplified Holy Compact Bible: Captures the Full Meaning behind the Original Greek and Hebrew*. 2015. Grand Rapids, Michigan: Zondervan.

Ref 5   Walter, John H, Victor Harold Matthews, and Mark William Chavalas. 2000. *The IVP Bible Background Commentary of the Old Testament*. Downers Grove, Ill. Intervarsity Press.

Ref 6   Genesis 6:14 *Spiritual Warfare Bible*. 2012. Lake Mary, Florida, Charisma House.

Ref 7   Exodus 2:4 *Amplified Holy Compact Bible: Captures the Full Meaning behind the Original Greek and Hebrew*. 2015. Grand Rapids, Michigan: Zondervan.

Ref 8   Google search. Question 'What was the use of bitumen in ancient times?'

Ref 9   Alec, Wendy. *Visions from Heaven* 2014. Warboys Publishing, Ireland.

Ref 10   John 14:16-18. *Amplified Holy Compact Bible: Captures the Full Meaning behind the Original Greek and Hebrew*. 2015. Grand Rapids, Michigan: Zondervan.

Ref 11   Johnson, Bill. 2019. *The Resting Place: Living immersed in the presence of God*. Shippensburg, Pa: Destiny Image Publishers, Inc.

Ref 12   Cron, Lisa. 2016. *Story Genius: How to use brain science to go beyond outlining and write a riveting novel (before you Waste Three Years Writing 327 Pages That Go Nowhere)*. Berkeley: Ten Speed Press.

Ref 13   Mark 5:35-42 *Amplified Holy Compact Bible: Captures the Full Meaning behind the Original Greek and Hebrew*. 2015. Grand Rapids, Michigan: Zondervan.

CHAPTER FIVE

Safe Passage

'It's time to make a difference.' [1]
JENTEZEN FRANKLIN

In the last chapter, we left our strong, feisty, fearless leader, Miriam, standing some distance away on the bank of the Nile River waiting to find out what would happen to her baby brother. Her mother, Jochebed, had carefully prepared the basket and covered it with tar and pitch to make it as watertight as possible. As a mother myself, I believe Jochebed would have covered the weaved vessel that carried her precious cargo down the river with so much more than sticky bitumen. She would have covered and coated that basket with a thick layer of fierce and fervent prayer because Pharaoh's malevolent plan had now propelled Jochebed and Miriam to take a huge risk and do something others would not be willing to do. Like the two midwives Shiphrah and Puah, this mother and daughter duo were warriors in the making. The plan was to send this special baby along the Nile River rather than send him into the depths of a watery grave, and this plan, God's plan, was non-negotiable.

They knew that even though the Egyptians considered Pharaoh a god, as far as these two warrior women were concerned, he was just a man whose scheme wasn't going to stop God or His people from rising up.

I believe the determination young Miriam showed in making sure her baby brother would be safely carried along the river was pivotal in her development and growth as a warrior. 'His sister stood at a distance to see what would happen to him'[2] Keeping her eyes on her brother was now Miriam's number one mission as she observed her mother place him into the prepared basket amongst the reeds along the Nile River ready for the current to carry him. Although just a child herself, Miriam needed to make sure her view of the basket wasn't hindered along the banks, so she guarded and secured a safe passage for her brother with her watchful, sharp, twenty-twenty vision until his rescuer was in sight.

Do What Must Be Done

It's important to slow this transition down in Miriam's rising as I believe this was where the warrior was truly formed and shaped in our brave leader. Imagine with me, just for a moment, if Miriam's mother, Jochebed, hadn't really believed in her young daughter that day? Do you think Miriam would have found the courage to rise up to the challenge?

I highly doubt it.

Jochebed clearly knew her daughter well. She knew her personality traits inside and out.

Let me ask you a question. Do you know your number on an enneagram? When you do, it's very enlightening to find out your traits and quirks in what makes you tick. Of course, we shall never know Jochebed's enneagram number, but from the scraps of evidence I've gathered in this part of Miriam's story, I feel she'd be an eight. One of the character traits of the challenger is, 'don't mess with the people I love' and Jochebed's courage, mixed with her intelligence and stamina [3] sent a red, hot message to a cold-hearted fool named Pharaoh that he had unwittingly unleashed a mama bear whose righteous indignation was neither hot nor cold but just right.

It was time to

rise up,

make a difference,

take a stand,

and the responsibility to carry out the second phase of the plan now rested on Miriam's young shoulders. It was imperative that she believed in herself just as much as her mother did. We need to realise, that as we move through the transitions in our journey, God guides us through each one of our uncomfortable transitional junctures because He knows us so well. In fact, He knows us inside and out. And as we grow out of the ashes into our warrior status, He gives us more and more responsibility because He whole-heartedly believes we have the capability to rise. I mean, if it was up to us, we'd choose easy street, right? The short cut that avoids all those fiery, fearful, unpleasant transitional moments in our stories. The painless route that gets us to warrior status far quicker than the hot, furnace of the dry, dusty road that helps prepare us for our future wilderness experience. However, if you're looking for fast, microwaveable moments along this journey as you transition through each stage of reigniting the warrior within, then I'm afraid God is going to go all Gordon Ramsey on you, and, just like the famous chef, He will tell you that microwaves can't achieve 'the texture, the searing, and the contrast' that the slow burn a stove offers.[4] Quick-fix microwavable steps are fine if you want to become a warrior who resembles a plate of re-heated leftovers. However, you, dear friend, need to become the warrior whose very presence shows balance, incandescent, distinction rather than looking like an afterthought that gets served up with no finesse. If we keep choosing to hide away from the slow process of the flames then our Phoenix wings will not be shaped and formed properly, and misshaped wings don't have the strength to rise from the ashes. As Erwin McManus states, 'The warrior is not formed by what has been done and what can't be done; the heart of the warrior is formed by what must be done.'[5] I believe, Miriam's Phoenix wings were not shaped and formed by what Pharaoh had done, or by what she was told couldn't be done, but by what *must* be done. To become a warrior you cannot dodge, bypass, evade, sidestep, or shun the slow transitional moments in this journey otherwise your wings will stay stumpy lumps on those shoulders of yours because you've not allowed them to be shaped and formed with the slow burn of responsibility that the follow-up shot requires.

Wings

Let's continue with Miriam's story…

'Then Pharaoh's daughter went down to the Nile to bathe, and her attendants were walking along the riverbank. She saw the basket among the reeds and sent her slave girl to get it. She opened it and saw the baby. He was crying, and she felt sorry for him. "This is one of the Hebrew babies," she said. Then the sister asked Pharaoh's daughter, "Shall I go and get one of the Hebrew women to nurse the baby for you?" "Yes, go," she answered. And the girl went and got the baby's mother. Pharaoh's daughter said to her, "Take this baby and nurse him for me, and I will pay you." So, the woman took the baby and nursed him. When the child grew older, she took him to Pharaoh's daughter, and he became her son. She named him Moses, saying, "I drew him out of the water".'[6]

It seems that God is almost mocking the unsympathetic fool Pharaoh as He makes sure that his sympathetic daughter takes in and cares for the Hebrew baby boy that, by all accounts, should have been thrown into the Nile. Either Pharaoh understood he was never going to win the argument with his daughter about keeping the baby because he knew that when she set her mind on something she could be just as stubborn as her mother, or he decided to turn a blind eye to the new edition to his family that had sailed into his world in a bitumen coated basket. We shall never know those details, but one thing is clear, Miriam became proficient and efficient in her follow-up shot helping her to rise from the ashen pit of Pharaoh's plan and step up to the challenge God was needing her to do. As she boldly asks Pharaoh's daughter if she could go and find a Hebrew woman to nurse the baby for her, Miriam did what was required because, as far as she was concerned, it was God's perfect plan and not Pharaoh's relentless unrest that was going to succeed. This characteristic of trusting God even in the face of opposition was a sign of a true warrior in the making, and as Miriam opened up her fresh Phoenix wings against the winds of adversity, she knew that God was teaching her how to fly.[7]

Why Do You Hide?

Miriam's emerging from her hiding place and approaching Pharaoh's daughter helped her to rise up. This, I believe, was an important transitional moment not only in her brother's journey of who he was going to become but in her own journey. A safe passage of protection from God was needed as He was starting to prepare, shape and develop Miriam's wings as she learned the ways of the warrior. The hiding theme seems to transfer in the story from Jochebed hiding her baby boy until she could no longer keep him to her hidden daughter, Miriam, along the banks of the Nile. There is something to be aware of as you learn to use your fresh, new wings in your journey of rising. Someone else is watching and waiting for the perfect opportune moment for you to come out from your hiding place and start flapping your wings. His name is Satan, and as your enemy knows, once you experience flight, those wings of yours are going to take you to new places that you could never have reached before you had them. I know in my own reigniting of the warrior within the enemy has used his intimidating scare tactics that have caused me to draw back, retreat and stay hidden. For the most part, his schemes have worked in my life, as it seemed every time I found a morsel of confidence and decided to open up my wings and start to rise into the freedom of my position and authority in leadership, I would find myself fledgling and fluttering around like a little, lost bird, intimidated by others because all their stares, tuts and shaking heads taught me to question my calling. I mean, who was I to step into my God-given authority and become an influential leader? So, I would quickly draw back and hide, returning to the slavery of fear I had come from.

The enemy's schemes started to really ramp up and take shape in my life when I was fifteen and a preacher prophesied over me in a church service one evening, telling me that God had his hand on me for a purpose, for leadership so I could be used to win many others to Christ. Within a few weeks of receiving that prophecy, I found myself being verbally abused by my pastor in the church foyer after a service. That demoralising moment caused me to shrink back and run for many years from the calling God has placed on my life until I grasped how to develop the strength my wings needed to keep flying. I've had to learn how to hide differently, in the refuge of the secret place where God has showed me His Truth against the lies of the enemy as I place my confidence in who He says that I am. Even now, the enemy tries his best to steal, kill, and destroy my God-given authority so my leadership is decreased and diminished. As John Bevere points out, 'If you don't walk in your God-given authority, someone will take it from you and use it against you'[8] and I have learned to become wise to the enemy's schemes because when you stay hidden because of fear and not hidden in God's strength, your wings become underdeveloped and weak so you cannot soar into all He has planned for you.

Your enemy knows if he can get you to retreat, draw back and hide you'll have no strength to come forward, step up and rise into your God-given authority. Believe me, the fear of man over the fear of God intimidates you by keeping you in your hiding place so you don't take a stand. It makes me so mad in knowing the fact that I've wasted too many years worrying about whether other people are going to give me permission to fly. Wounded warriors who have experienced rejection, isolation and humiliation get used to hiding, and hiding warriors suit the enemy's plans perfectly because he knows suppressing the authority of a warrior disarms the follow-up shot and renders it useless.

It was essential for Miriam to leave her hiding place along the riverbanks and rise above her current circumstances so she could test her flight feathers. Her confidence in the leader God had called her to be and the authority He had given to her came from a hiding place she knew she needed to rest in, and it secured a safe passage in the transition of developing her wings as she learned the ways of the warrior. Although the story doesn't detail how Miriam actually felt when she approached Pharaoh's daughter, we can assume that for one so young, she could have felt intimidated by her power and position, knowing that her father was the one who had set into place the plan for her brother's demise. But Miriam knew she had been called for a greater purpose than to stay hidden amongst the reeds along the banks of the Nile River. The reignited warrior within Miriam wasn't going to wait for permission from Pharaoh to approach his daughter and leverage her compassion to help her brother live.

Psalm 91 is known as the 'soldiers' prayer' because the alleged story goes that every day in World War I the 91st Brigade recited Psalm 91 for their protection. Amazingly, the unit that had the same number as the Psalm, didn't suffer a single combat death, unlike other units did in that war.[9] All sixteen of this Psalm's verses hold a power-packed punch to the enemy's game plan, however, I just wanted to highlight a few verses.

'When you sit enthroned under the shadow of Shaddai,
you are hidden in the strength of God Most High.
He's the hope that holds me and the Stronghold to shelter me,
the only God for me, and my great confidence.

He will rescue you from every hidden trap of the enemy,
and He will protect you from false accusation and deadly curse.
His massive arms are wrapped around you, protecting you.
You can run under his covering of majesty and hide,
His arms of faithfulness are a shield keeping you from harm...
When we live our lives within the shadow of God Most High,
our secret hiding place, we will always be shielded from
harm.'[10]

The reason you exist, my dear friend, is because something needs to be done, and if you're this far into the book in learning how to reignite the warrior within, then you have the determination and the resoluteness to see it through. Miriam teaches us to run under the covering of God's majesty because our true hiding place isn't along the banks of the river but *in* God, and when you are given the space to spread your wings, then your confidence in your God-given authority is going to soar.

Liberated

There is a sense of freedom when you break free from the shackles of hiding. Interestingly, the name Mary in Greek is Miriam[11] and from the pages of Miriam's story in the Old Testament to Mary, mother of Jesus in the New, these two women are connected to great deliverers and both watched over them in their young lives when they were in danger of wicked kings. They didn't allow power-crazy people to cause them to shrink back in fear by letting their intimidation tactics stop them from rising and using their wings. Miriam and Mary had learned to hide in God and not in their circumstances. And whether it was a Pharaoh who ruled over Egypt, or a king named, Herod, it didn't matter because their choice was the same. They could either choose to go back toward the safety of hiding or move forward toward growth and become the warriors God intended. As warriors, they knew they had to keep choosing growth over fear time and time again.[12] The enemy wants to keep us in the confined spaces of our thinking, believing his lies that we're too ill-equipped, too weak, and too powerless to fight back in the authority God has given to us. For our enemy knows that in our cramped, imprisoned condition it will only stunt our growth and eventually the lack of oxygen will snuff out the flame within us. We've all heard of the fight or flight response, but what if we used our new set of wings to confidently go from fight to flight mode that will propel us upwards! Listen, my friend, if fear is causing you to hide from your calling because you feel too scared to rise up into the warrior God has called you to become, then let the words of Marianne Williamson encourage you to rise up.

'We ask ourselves, who am I to be brilliant, gorgeous, talented, fabulous? Actually, who are you not to be? You are a child of God. Playing it small does not serve the world. There's nothing enlightened about shrinking so that other people won't feel insecure around you… We were born to manifest the glory of God that is within us… And as we let our own light shine, we unconsciously give other people permission to do the same. As we're liberated from our own fear, our presence automatically liberates others.'[13]

Don't allow the enemy to back you into a corner and leave you on the ropes. It's time to make a difference. You're a warrior who is brilliant, gorgeous, talented, and fabulous. Stop playing it small. Stop hiding in the shadows that incarcerate and confine you because your liberation will liberate others!

Endnotes: Chapter Five

Ref 1   Franklin, Jentezen. 2017. *Right people Right place Right plan: Discerning the voice of God.* Whitaker House.

Ref 2   Exodus 2:4 Syswerda, Jean, and Faith Organization.2001. NIV Women of Faith Study Bible: New International Version. Grand Rapids, Mich.: Zondervan.

Ref 3   Cron, Ian Morgan, and Suzanne Stabile. 2016. *The Road back to You: An enneagram journey to self-discovery.* Ivp Books.

Ref 4   Google search question 'Why does Gordon Ramsay hate microwaves?'

Ref 5   Erwin Raphael McManus. 2019. *The Way Of The Warrior: An Ancient Path To Inner Peace.* New York: Waterbrook.

Ref 6   Exodus 2:5-10 Syswerda, Jean, and Faith Organization.2001. NIV Women of Faith Study Bible: New International Version. Grand Rapids, Mich.: Zondervan.

Ref 7   Bevere, Lisa. 2020. *Godmothers: Why You Need One. How to Be One.* Grand Rapids, Mich.: Revell.

Ref 8   Bevere, John. 1995. *Breaking Intimidation: How to overcome fear and release the gifts of God in your life.* Charisma House.

Ref 9   Google search question: 'Why is psalm 91 called the soldiers prayer?'

Ref 10   Psalm 91: 1- 4, Psalm 91:9, Psalm 91:14 The Passion Translation: New Testament with Psalms, Proverbs, and Song of Songs, Second Edition. Passion & Fire Ministries, Inc. Broadstreet Publishing: 2018.

Ref 11   John MacArthur YouTube Watch. 'The Leading Lady of The Exodus' sermon. Website: Youtube.com

Ref 12   Antciff, Amanda. 2010. *Women Rising: A challenge to stand up and step out into a life of influence.* Creation House.

Ref 13   Antciff, Amanda. 2010. *Women Rising: A challenge to stand up and step out into a life of influence.* Creation House.

CHAPTER SIX

Developed in the Dark

*'You make your messengers into winds of the Spirit
and all your ministers become flames of fire.'* [1]
PSALM 104:4 (TPT)

Now that I've got all up in your business about not shrinking back and making a difference. Now that you're all fired up because I mentioned the crucial transitional moment in Exodus 2, where Miriam learnt how to use the winds of adversity that taught her how to fly, I'm going to throw some cold water over you. The Bible does not mention our audacious, confident, warrior until she is an adult in Exodus chapter fifteen. Her two younger brothers, Aaron, and Moses get to play the lead roles in the narrative this time, guiding us through each careful step of the ten plagues of Egypt and how God brought the Israelites out of slavery. Yes, Miriam had another brother who was the first-born son to her parents, Jochebed and Amram. However, Aaron does not come into the story until Moses is begging God at the burning bush in Exodus

4:13 to send someone else on the suicidal, daring mission to convince Pharaoh to relent and let God's people go. '... please my Lord, send the message (of rescue to Israel) by (someone else,) whomever else You will (choose)." Then the anger of the Lord was kindled and burned against Moses; he said, "Is there not your brother, Aaron the Levite? I know that he speaks fluently."'[2] So, how did Aaron survive Pharaoh's ridiculous royal decree regarding first-born sons? The decree only concerned male babies after the vile plan was put into place[3] and this is possibly why Aaron dodged the murky waters of the Nile River. I have deliberately left Miriam's other brother, Aaron, aside for the first part of our journey as we will be getting to know him and his leadership style a little more as the Exodus story progresses. But for now, we are going to leave the path and venture underground into gaps and caves as this next phase and transition of reigniting the warrior within can only be developed in the dark.

So, what happened to our leader Miriam in between those thirteen chapters? Why does she only surface again in chapter fifteen? Miriam's emergence brought with it a new title to her resumé—prophetess. 'The prophetess, Miriam (Aaron's sister), picked up tambourine, and all the rest of the women followed her with tambourines and joyful dancing.'[4] Hold on, Miriam was just a girl when we left her along the banks of the Nile River, the one who was brave enough to not shrink back so that the connection between her mother, baby brother and the daughter of Pharaoh would take place. Now thirteen chapters have gone by and not even a whisper of her name throughout the iconic moments in the lead up to the Exodus out of Egypt. Each epic transitional moment all happened without a glance in Miriam's direction, and now suddenly, Miriam emerges once again in a later chapter and is called a prophetess whom other women follow? I'm curious to know how she reached this status. Thirteen chapters is a long time between drinks, and the gap in Miriam's story from learning how to use her fresh, Phoenix wings to becoming a prophetess whom women follow needs some careful reflection. What happened in the tedious long wait? How did this warrior woman earn the badge of female prophet? I believe, if we warriors are to learn anything from Miriam's life, then we need to pause here for a moment and glean all that we can from what she is about to share with us. This seems as good a spot as any in our journey to open up the Thermos, lean in and catch some wisdom over a cuppa.

Please Mind the Gap

Perhaps Miriam's anonymity helped in the early phases of her calling that taught her to rise well and keep in step with God's timing by allowing the transformation to come from the inside out rather than the outside, which allowed her leadership to have longevity. Well, that's wonderful to hear. However, while that statement is true, as God really does some of His best work from the inside out in all His warriors, what do we do when we find ourselves, like Miriam, in a gap within our stories? It would be hypocritical of me to say that I've never struggled with the divide between knowing what God had promised me and what my current circumstances look like. If you were offering me a job, you would notice plenty of gaps in my resumé. And I know, those gaps along the journey to rising can feel as wide as a ravine or as dark and deep as an abyss when you're in one. All those monotonous, mundane, everyday moments where you feel like

God hasn't even glimpsed your way because you believe He's too busy orchestrating everyone else's epic storyline that seems to be chock full of highlight reels while you're left alone in the dark. Miriam feels your pain. She too had to scroll through some of the best moments of her brothers lives while they did all the heavy lifting in getting the Israelites out from under the tyranny of Pharaoh's rule. Gaps can be as painful as they are long, and yet, they are necessary in reigniting the warrior within. So, what is the purpose of a gap? A 'gap exists because we are often not as big as the vision we carry. To fit and fulfill the dream we have to grow in character, capacity, and capability'[5] as Amanda Antciff so wisely states.

Grow in character?

Ugh.

Grow in capacity?

Ugh, ugh.

Grow in capability?

Ugh, ugh, UGH!

That seems like a lot of gaps.

Okay, I know, you were hoping for some inspiring scripture to keep you going while you're taking a break and sipping your tea.

Sorry.

Alright, if you insist, here's one for you. Habakkuk 2:3, 'For the vision points ahead to a time I have appointed; it testifies regarding the end, and it will not lie. Even if there is a delay, wait for it. It is coming and will come without delay.'[6] The vision and promises for your future will only come at the appointed, God-given time. There you go. Isn't that what you want to hear? Good things are coming. However, I hate to break it to you, but

Habakkuk still states that you have to... yes, that's correct... wait for it.

UGH!

Okay, what about a metaphor to cheer you up and help you understand the importance of gaps? I want you to think of your warrior status as a train pulling into a station and your standing on the platform waiting for the train to stop and open its doors so you can climb aboard. As the train pulls in, you look down at your feet and painted on the concrete of the platform in big, bold, yellow font, right in front of the automatic doors of the carriage you are ready to board, are the words, 'PLEASE MIND THE GAP'. To get on the train safely, you will need to stretch your legs over the gap that sits between the train and the platform, otherwise you'll fall right down into that hole, and that would be very dangerous for you.

Listen, dear warrior, God doesn't just want you to rise up, He wants you to *grow up* into a disciplined warrior and that can only come in God putting a few gaps into your story because He knows gaps make us stretch and step up into our destinies.[7] You feel the waiting in the gaps are not helping you to fly freely but are actually hindering your flight path. Waiting for anything can be hard. Nevertheless, the enemy is waiting too. Waiting for you to fall from a great height so that others question the authenticity of your faith. Growing up is what we need to do and only the gaps in our journey can stretch us enough so we grow in character, capacity, and capability to carry the vision and see it through to its God-appointed time because this is the way of a warrior. Miriam went from little girl to adult in the space of thirteen chapters and that required a lot of growing up! However, when she came back into the narrative, she was a prophetess and that only came because she learned how to mind the gaps.

Cave Dwellers

As we test out our wings and learn how to rise up from the ashes, we need to understand that God starts to work on our character, capacity, and capability when we decide to stop hiding from Him and find out what it means to become hidden in Him. This kind of hiding is so different from the hiding I speak about in my book, *Wounded and on the Run*. Staying hidden because you're reeling from the havoc and alienation that spiritual abuse, betrayal, or abandonment brings is like slapping on a Band-Aid and hoping it is going to dress and patch up those deep wounds. Many people are bleeding out because of the bullets and arrows that have been fired by the hunter, Satan, the accuser, for he takes great pleasure in following the blood trail that flows behind the wounded ones. However, this is not the sort of hiding I want to speak about here.

In my own Christian journey, I have found that staying hidden *in* Christ, as it says in Colossians 3:3, that is; my old life is now dead and gone and my new life is now concealed and covered by God,[8] helps shield and camouflage me from the dangers so many wounded warriors often fall back into. God, in His love, guides and leads His beloved warriors into the deepest, darkest caverns away from the glaring spotlight that can so easily blind us into serving from a fear-based leadership which is fuelled by the lighter fluid of performance and self-preservation rather than by the fire of God's presence, and that type of leadership is to be avoided at all costs. God needs His true warriors to become cave dwellers first. He needs to teach the techniques of how to tuck in our wings so we are able to navigate the turbulence found in the rising, otherwise we'll get blown off course and the enemy's shots will knock us out of the sky.

Before David rose as the next king of Israel, his Phoenix wings felt the full turbulence of Saul's jealousy towards his anointing which led him to become a cave dweller for many years until he finally took his place as Saul's predecessor. And yet, during David's reign, he had to stay hidden again, but this time it was from his own son, Absalom. David had learned so much about God, himself, and his leadership while hiding in those caves and this possibly helped him when his own son attempted to overthrow his kingdom. In 2 Samuel chapter 23, it says, 'Here are the last words of David, son of Jesse: the words of the one raised up, the anointed one of Jacob's True God, the sweet songwriter of Israel."[9] Once again, David found himself hiding in a cave, just as he did before he rose to the throne. 'At the beginning of harvest, these top three (warriors) of David's thirty chief warriors joined David at the cave of Adullam. A group of Philistines was camped in the valley of Rephaim, David was hiding in his safe place, and the main force of the Philistines was quartered in Bethlehem.'[10] In this chapter, David lists the warriors who fought battles with him by name. Josheb-basshebeth killed 800 in one battle. Eleazar stood his ground and didn't retreat. Shammah stood in the centre of a field of lentils and killed many Philistines.[11] These were David's top three honoured warriors; and yet, the list goes on and thirty mighty men of valour are individually named. I love how The Voice Translation says, 'these are the warriors who were counted.'[12] What about you, dear warrior? Will you allow God to stretch you in the gaps, just like He stretched Miriam? Are you willing to become a cave dweller like David so God can raise you up into your destiny? If you are then I guarantee you will become a warrior who will be counted. It's in these transitions, in the gaps, and in the caves where most of your developing is done. Dark places are what every would-be warrior needs to experience in their rising and the gaps is where God stretches them. This is so that their follow-up shot can be wielded well. For it is in those dark places, the gaps of transition where true warriors become fully on fire for God.

Endnotes: Chapter Six

Ref 1   Psalm 104:4 The Passion Translation: New Testament with Psalms, Proverbs, and Song of Songs, Second Edition. Passion & Fire Ministries, Inc. Broadstreet Publishing: 2018.

Ref 2   Exodus 4:13-14 *Amplified Holy Compact Bible: Captures the Full Meaning behind the Original Greek and Hebrew.* 2015. Grand Rapids, Michigan: Zondervan.

Ref 3   Google Question 'How did Aaron (Moses' brother) survive being slaughtered when Pharaoh killed the first-born sons of Israelites?' Website: Bible.org.

Ref 4   Exodus 15:20 Ecclesia Bible Society. 2012. *The Voice Bible: Step into the Story of Scripture.* Nashville: Thomas Nelson

Ref 5   Antciff, Amanda. 2010. *Women Rising: A challenge to stand up and step out into a life of influence.* Creation House.

Ref 6   Habakkuk 2:3 Ecclesia Bible Society. 2012. *The Voice Bible: Step into the Story of Scripture.* Nashville: Thomas Nelson

Ref 7   Antciff, Amanda. 2010. *Women Rising: A challenge to stand up and step out into a life of influence.* Creation House.

Ref 8   Colossians 3:3 Ecclesia Bible Society. 2012. *The Voice Bible: Step into the Story of Scripture.* Nashville: Thomas Nelson

Ref 9   2 Samuel 23:1 Ecclesia Bible Society. 2012. *The Voice Bible: Step into the Story of Scripture.* Nashville: Thomas Nelson

Ref 10   2 Samuel 23:13-14 Ecclesia Bible Society. 2012. *The Voice Bible: Step into the Story of Scripture.* Nashville: Thomas Nelson

Ref 11   2 Samuel 23:8-11 Ecclesia Bible Society. 2012. *The Voice Bible: Step into the Story of Scripture.* Nashville: Thomas Nelson

Ref 12   2 Samuel 23:24 Ecclesia Bible Society. 2012. *The Voice Bible: Step into the Story of Scripture.* Nashville: Thomas Nelson

CHAPTER SEVEN

Stick to the Plan

'Sometimes, you just have to jump and hope to God the net appears. As everything inside you screams, That it's now! The time is here.' [1]
BILL MITTON

Perhaps after the last chapter you're feeling less enthusiastic about reigniting the warrior within. Maybe you're still thinking our conversation through that we had over a cuppa about gaps, caves, growing up and stretching that finds the excitement you felt in the ash pile, scented with cinders and soot. Now you're wondering if you'll ever gain enough confidence to catch the updraft so you're able to spread your wings, soaring and circling as you fly away from the ashes and into better days. However, as we rinse out our camping cups in the freshwater stream and pack away the Thermos, Miriam cautions you that the path of a warrior is not for the faint of heart. She reminds you that when you left the safety of the little cabin in the forest and signed up for this journey of reigniting the warrior within it was going to be no walk in the park. She points out that for your follow-up shot to be pitch perfect, for the notes to sound out toward the enemy and hit him where it hurts, you'll need to surrender once again and lay down your own agenda, just like you did when Jesus healed your wounds. Remember that moment when you finally decided to stop running? When you chose to walk through the narrow door of the little, wooden cabin and submit to His gentle care as He cleaned and dressed your wounds? Do you recall the part when you surrendered to Him completely and became helpless in His nail-scarred hands?

For the Phoenix to be resurrected it first needs to die in the flames and become helpless in the fire. Jesus talks about His own surrender when He tells His disciples, Philip, and Andrew in John 12:24 that 'unless a grain of wheat is planted in the ground and dies, it remains a solitary seed. But when it is planted, it produces in death a great harvest.'[2] As warriors rising, are we willing to commit to this journey of reignition and die to ourselves so we 'feel His warm resurrection breath across the flickering chambers of our hearts'[3] as Ann Voskamp so poetically puts, so that we, the wounded ones, the overcomers who have felt the sting of abandonment, decide right in this moment, to say we are going to live fully abandoned to our Saviour and give Him our all because He was the One who gave us His all?

I do hope so.

If you decide to turn back now, dear friend, your song of freedom will not ring true because for your follow-up shot to be successful you need to keep going. You need to embrace the long gaps, the deep, dark caves, and the painful stretching as these are all an essential part of your growth. Think of them as a soundcheck, a key preparation time for God to make a few adjustments as He finely tunes your character, capacity, and capability so you're able to plug into the amplifier and pump up the volume on your song that is rising, letting the enemy hear it loud and clear. Goodness knows he has tried his best to decrease the sound of your follow-up shot over the years by badly wounding you so that you stay muted. However, he cannot wound with his poisonous arrows of abandonment when you've chosen to live completely abandoned. For he knows that we have made it this far in our journey and we are not backing down or backing out now.

Walk-In Wardrobe

As I mentioned before, if you offered me a job, you'd find plenty of gaps in my resumé, and for a few years I was a stay-at-home mum to my two children. It was during those years, in between school drop offs, teaching the values of our faith, and making sure the house ran smoothly while my husband worked shifts that I discovered I could write. I signed up for a correspondence course that taught how to write for children and my tutor told me that my assignments were well-constructed, the pacing was spot on and a pleasure to read. She said that my writing had a lot of potential because it was clear and concise. Looking back, I can join the dots as to why God was leading me to writing, and apart from being an avid reader and my love of stationary, (who doesn't love a beautiful notebook and a shiny new pen, right?!) I wanted to take what my tutor said in her feedback seriously. So, I set about in finding a desk so I could write my first bestseller.

After searching for a few weeks, we found the perfect one in an op shop. It was an old-fashioned wooden desk with lots of drawers and compartments that would keep my new workspace neat and tidy. Although the desk was fairly cheap, my bargain mindset automatically kicked in, as we were living on one wage—and I really wanted that desk—so I cheekily haggled a little with the price. After a short pause, the lady volunteering in the shop finally relented to my asking price. We lived in a small house where all three bedrooms were taken and there was no room for a 'writer's' office. I tried lots of places and spaces where my desk should go and none of them worked. I was either too easily distracted or I was being constantly interrupted by my two young children wanting to know what I was doing, what I was writing and why. That was until a thought popped into my head one day. What if my desk could fit into our walk-in wardrobe? I looked at our wardrobe in our bedroom, it was no bigger than the size of a small cupboard and so I measured the door frame and the width of my desk. Yes, it would fit. Just. I set to work and dragged my desk into that tiny space, excited that was where I was going to write my first children's novel.

My family thought I'd gone crazy as I sat in the walk-in wardrobe, typing words out on my laptop day after day. Although cramped and feeling slightly claustrophobic, I managed to close the door of our walk-in wardrobe when my family was fed, watered and happy and write non-stop for a few hours. I used to smile to myself when I heard one of my children occasionally ask their dad where mum had gone and go searching around the house for me. 'She's in the cupboard writing, so don't disturb her' my husband would tell them as I tapped away at the keys putting one word in front of the other until one day, I had created a finished manuscript. I was so proud.

However, I would love to tell you that the first publishing house I sent my manuscript to couldn't wait to sign me up and offer me a contract, but that would be totally untrue because they didn't. In fact, neither did the next publishing house, nor the next, or the next one after that. In the writers' kingdom publishers are known as the gatekeepers, and for good reason as it seemed all those years of writing page after page, word after word I was going to get no help in them giving me the key so I could open up the gate in getting my work published. I felt totally discouraged and disappointed. I wondered whether I should continue in the pursuit of becoming an author or call it a day on my dream. Honestly, even for an introvert writer, it was getting really lonely sitting in my dimly lit walk-in wardrobe month after month trying to write something worthy of being printed. Thankfully, one of my friends knew another writer who had just published her first book and after attending her book launch, she invited me to a Christian writers' conference to keep my writing embers burning. While there, something reignited within me, and after the writers' conference there was a flame that couldn't be distinguished no matter how many rejection letters or knockbacks I'd received. I'd been through the gaps and the caves, learning my craft in those hidden moments and now nothing could snuff out my determination in getting published regardless of how long it would take. There was something about writing that my soul kept circling around and it just would not let me go. When I questioned God about whether I was going in the right direction, whether to turn around, head back and give up altogether, He'd keep telling me the same four words,

'Stick to the plan'.

Fast forward seventeen years and you'd shake my hand and pat me on the back as your eyes scanned my resumé. You'll be impressed that I eventually found a publisher and wrote my first book, wrote many, many blog posts and recorded heaps of podcasts that have helped many people to become set free. And yet, none of that would have happened if I hadn't done something crazy, something so ridiculous in dragging my desk into my walk-in wardrobe, sitting my butt in my chair regardless of my circumstances and write. I have to say, that children's novel I wrote may possibly never see the light of day, as my debut book was adult non-fiction and not children's fiction. However, it was in the gaps and the dark caves where I learned not to quit, when the road to becoming a published author became tough and hard, where I found my identity as a writer and to write the messages that burned in my heart. None of those hours and hours of development in the gaps and caves were ever wasted on God.

To be honest, I've wanted to turn back so many times in my writing journey. I wanted to run into the safety of a nine to five job more than once, with its open, welcoming arms that would give me the promise of stability going straight into my bank account on a weekly basis. I've practically begged God for an escape in my call to write, for me to just live a normal life and forget about all this living by faith stuff. However, each time I stray from the crucible, He marches me right back into the flames until all my bridges connected to safer paths have been completely burned. Theologian, A.W. Tozer, speaks of this dilemma when he says, 'As long as you can run and go to safety, you are not in God's hands. As long as you can back out, as long as there is a bridge behind you, you can retreat. As Christians, we want to follow God, but we also want a second plan in case it doesn't work out.'[4] I don't know about you, but I want to live my life in His hands, and all those gaps, every unseen, unapplauded moment in my writing, sitting at my desk in my cave-like walk-in wardrobe so I could write uninterrupted when my kids were small, keeps reminding me to stick to the plan because God didn't want me to settle for less than His best for me. God doesn't want that for you either, dear friend. Why settle for believable, achievable mediocrity[5] that keeps you hiding instead of rising up? Why fan the flames of fear so you live small, limited, and contained because you fear the unknown? Part of my frustrations in reigniting the warrior within have been because I didn't choose to fully commit to God's plan for my life. I have always mapped out a plan B just in case. However, God made it quite clear that there was no plan B and there never was. Simply stick to the plan and trust Him with the process because if we do we'll make it through.

Don't Look Back

For the Phoenix to rise once again, it needs to commit to the process of the fire as it sheds the old self and brings forth the new. Hebrews 12:29 talks about God being 'like a fierce fire that consumes everything'[6] and over the past couple of years, since the global pandemic, I have not only found myself changing and being consumed by His fire but I have also witnessed my close circle of friends not allow the heat of the challenges they've faced get the better of them. I can honestly say that our friendship has become tighter than a grandmother's perm as we've embraced, committed, and surrendered to God's transforming fire and the plan He has for each one of our lives. It hasn't been easy. Not by a long shot, however, through the flames we have all risen and learned how to reach in and lean on each other's strength during the process and in turn, reach out and lean on God's strength more and more and more as He raises His warriors, so that the follow-up shot is cocked and ready to be fired straight at the enemy. Isaiah 43:2 says, 'If it seems like you're walking through fire with flames licking at your limbs, keep going; you won't be burned'[7] and you will not be burned, dear friend, I promise you.

Thinking over the prophesy I was given when I was fifteen, about the mantle of leadership on my life and the responsibility it carried, I didn't have the maturity to carry out the plan God had for me let alone stick with it. I had a lot of maturing, stretching, and growing up to do in the fire of God's presence before I could rise up out from the ashes and fulfill my calling. Like I said before, we love the rising part of the Phoenix story but that only comes when we stick to the plan God has for us no matter how misunderstood, misinterpreted or misrepresented we feel. You need to keep moving forward in your journey because Miriam will tell you that looking back at Egypt only brings all manner of heartbreaks and this is why she urges you to surrender to the flames that reignite the warrior within and keep you looking forward. The slave-mentality clung to the Israelites thinking like the sticky tar found on the outside of Moses' basket, causing them to wander and wonder if God was with them until the fire of God refined them enough to step into the Promised Land.

You're wondering if you're cut out to become a warrior, as you battle with self-doubt. Well, I can tell you that I have had internal wars with self-doubt over the years and believe me it is no help when we need to stick to the plan. Our brave warrior, Miriam, possibly battled with self-doubt when she was hiding along the banks of the Nile River, waiting for the right moment to approach Pharaoh's daughter and do what her mother had asked her to do. The fear Miriam and her mother would have experienced while sticking to the plan is not recorded in

Scripture, and yet, the moment Miriam approached Pharaoh's daughter mirrors the part in the Exodus story when Moses needed to approach Pharaoh so God's people could walk toward their freedom. Throughout our journey, God may call us to rise up and boldly approach the gatekeepers, the ones who we deem to have all the power to stop our progress. Nevertheless, if we want to rise up and reignite the warrior within, we have to stick to the plan, trust God and do what He's called us to do because no gatekeeper is going to stop your follow-up shot. Once you understand the value of the fire you will not fear it. Commit to the plan, stick to it like glue otherwise they'll be no 'get up' in your go.

Trust me, dear warrior, you've got this!

Endnotes: Chapter Seven

Ref 1   Bill Mitton. 'A Leap Of Faith' PoemHunter.com November 4, 2011.

Ref 2   John 12:24 Ecclesia Bible Society. 2012. *The Voice Bible: Step into the Story of Scripture.* Nashville: Thomas Nelson

Ref 3   Voskamp, Ann. 2022. *Waymaker : Finding the Way to the Life You've Always Dreamed Of.* Nashville, Tennessee: W Publishing Group, An Imprint Of Thomas Nelson.

Ref 4   Tozer, A.W. and James L. Snyder. 2020. *The Fire Of God's Presence :Drawing near to a Holy God.* Grand Rapids: Bethany House Publishers.

Ref 5   Furtick, Steven. 2018. *(Un) Qualified: How God Uses Broken People to Do Big Things.* Colorado Springs, Colorado: Multnomah Books.

Ref 6   Hebrews 12:29 Ecclesia Bible Society. 2012. *The Voice Bible: Step into the Story of Scripture.* Nashville: Thomas Nelson

Ref 7   Isaiah 43:2 Ecclesia Bible Society. 2012. *The Voice Bible: Step into the Story of Scripture.* Nashville: Thomas Nelson

CHAPTER EIGHT

Stop the Crying!

'Weep if you must, then rise and lift your voice in song.' [1]
LISA BEVERE

So far in this first leg of our journey, we have learned the elements of courage, confidence, and the importance of allowing God to develop our character in the gaps and caves as these are all a crucial part of the warrior path that leads us through the difficulties the ancient Exodus road demands. These character traits are the sure foundation that will not only strengthen our wings as we learn how to fly free from the ashes of our past but will help us to arise and fully live out the resurrected life. But before we move on to the next phase of reigning the warrior within, I want to turn our focus onto Pharaoh's daughter for just a moment, as I believe she can help in one more aspect of a warrior's rising, and it is something that can often be overlooked in the follow-up shot. Apart from the fact she was the daughter to the most powerful man in Egypt, and regardless of the moment she felt sorry for the crying baby in the basket, took him in as her own son and named him, Moses, even though this noble woman knew full well he wasn't an Egyptian baby, this rebel princess chose to rise above the systemised way her father, Pharaoh, did things and decided that she was not going to join his cruel agenda. Many attempts from interpreters over the years have tried to name this unnamed daughter of the king of Egypt, as they have drawn their conclusions and cast their lots in joining the dots, trying their best to figure out what kind of woman she was. Still, one character trait of this warrior woman needs no theological excavation because Exodus 2: 5-6 confirms it. 'Pharaoh's daughter noticed the basket wedged among the reeds and wondered what it might contain. So, she instructed her maid to bring it to her. When Pharaoh's daughter opened the basket, she found the baby boy. He was crying, and her heart melted with compassion.'[2] Did you catch that? The daughter of a brutal, cruel dictator was a... comforter? Yes, and I find her kindness and affection toward others who are less fortunate than herself too irresistible to ignore.

Aerodynamic Lift

Compassion is not normally a word we would associate with the word 'warrior'. When we think of a warrior we think of a champion, a fighter, and a battler, but not a sympathiser, a consoler, or dare I say it, a friend. However, if we are to follow in Miriam's footsteps through the Exodus narrative, we need to get a handle on the act of compassion for it flows in the act of someone's transformation. If we look at the Exodus story, we find empathy and compassion become the keys to each intervention in the transformation of Moses. It happens two times setting Moses up on his warrior path toward freedom. The first, Pharaoh's daughter, and the second time is God Himself. We see divine intervention from God's compassion for His people as He commissioned Moses for his calling at the burning bush. Exodus 3:7-8 is when God speaks to Moses from the fiery shrub and says, 'I have seen how My people in Egypt are being mistreated. I have heard their groaning when the slave drivers torment and harass them; for I know well their suffering. I have come to rescue them from the oppression of the Egyptians, to lead them from that land where they are slaves and to give them a good land—a wide, open space flowing with milk and honey.'[3]

To rise up into all God has called us to be there has to be points in our lives where we need a compassionate intervention to make possible what was otherwise impossible.[4] It was the daughter's warmth from her compassion that helped deliver the Hebrew baby from the cold, dark waters of the Nile and it was the suffering of His people that ignited God's compassion and appointed Moses to be their deliverer. As Walter Brueggemann says, 'Israel's story is the flight from there to here'[4] and God's divine compassion propelled and carried the air upward into an aerodynamic lift, so His people were elevated from the ashes of Egypt's slavery and into the freedom of the land that flowed with milk and honey. Although the Exodus story is centred around the journey of Moses becoming a deliverer, the narrative is about the many and not just the one[5] and God's compassion is far reaching.

Getting back to Pharaoh's daughter, she could have possibly doubted her father's preposterous plan to murder all Hebrew male babies right from the get-go and stubbornly refused to join in his madness. Or perhaps she was unable to have children of her own and when she saw the miracle baby among the reeds she seized the opportunity with both hands and let the warmth of her compassion raise the Hebrew child up into a place of honour in Egypt, choosing the path to nurture and protect over her father's death and destruction detour. Regardless of her motive, God's plan was to save a group of people with His mercy and compassion that would change their lives forever. I love how God used no less than five women to position Moses where he needed to be to fulfill his calling. Shiphrah and Puah, the two midwives who delivered him safely, Jochebed, his mother, who prepared the basket so it floated safely down the Nile River, Miriam, his older sister, who kept a watchful eye on her baby brother so he was safely carried along the water, and Pharaoh's daughter, who's compassion intervention made the impossible possible. God certainly knew what He was doing when He chose each woman to play her part in the narrative of the Exodus story. And I believe it was the collective warmth of their compassion that created the powerful updraft, the aerodynamic lift of legacy that help raise a warrior named, Moses, whose compassion and care for God's people propelled him from the ashes and into his destiny some forty years later.

A Measure of Compassion

'We need to be careful that we don't get too indulgent with our wounding.' This truth bomb was epically said by my friend after reading my book, *Wounded and on the Run,* and I found myself nodding enthusiastically in total agreement with her. With all this warm-hearted, sympathetic compassionate talk that is helping your wings pick up speed as you learn to rise from the ashes, I need to highlight a warning sign up ahead, just in case you miss it and your wings get all caught up in the warm currents of grace and sympathy, and before you know it, you'll end up freefalling off a cliff into oblivion. Compassion is good, however, too much compassion brings with it a gravitational pull that is so strong it can drag you right back into the cinders of a slave mentality and eventually snuff out the embers that need to ignite the warrior within.

Ever heard of Compassion fatigue? It's when you become so emotionally and physically exhausted that you lose the ability to empathise. [6] Warrior be warned; I don't want your fire within to burnout because of Compassion fatigue. Burnout isn't where you want to end up, trust me, I've been there and it's not pretty. When you've been wounded you become starved of love and affection and for many years it can feel like a slow, lingering death. You know all too well what a lack of compassion feels like and you don't want others to experience what you've been through.

There are so many wounded, broken people in desperate need of the nourishment a good bowl of hearty compassion serves up, and that's okay because I've been malnourished myself and needed the compassion someone offered me to warm my soul and lift my spirits up. But as my friend so wisely pointed out, we can become too indulgent in our wounds and stuff ourselves silly with all the attention compassion gives to us, putting the fondness of friendship far higher than God which will only set us up for a fall. Like all nutrition, we need a healthy balance of empathy and compassion, and warriors learn to measure out their compassion wisely in relation to others so their intimacy with God comes first.

He wants you, dear warrior, to experience intimacy with Him as you personally encounter His practical wisdom that was gained from what you have observed, encountered, and undergone in your relationship with Him. God told me in the prophecy spoken over me when I was fifteen that He needs His love and compassion to come to a place where no friend, nor nobody else can understand, for He is the only One who can give us the sustenance and meet us in our deep longing to be known, to be loved, and to feel like we belong. He wants the same for you. 'For too long we've felt like the seventh grader in the school cafeteria, (hoping for a good scoop of compassion from other people) as we saw plenty of seats at the table but we soon discovered that there was no seat for us'.[7] And this is why we have hidden in the dark covering of the forest trees for so long, nursing our wounds from the cruelty of others whose rejection stung like a poison-tipped arrow that was aimed straight at our hearts. Know this, dear warrior, God sees you and He desires communion with you and when you feel His compassion then that is all you long for. As Sister Miriam James Heidland so wonderfully states, 'It's so delightful to be known'[7] and oh how true that is to have a deep friendship with Jesus, the One who's scars heal our deepest wounds as He draws us ever closer to Himself.

God's Chosen Instrument

Titling this chapter, 'Stop the crying!' now makes no sense as the last part you just read possibly made you cry. I'm sorry. Miriam is now searching in the backpack for a tissue. It's okay, don't keep those tears all bottled up, for God has taken note of your journey so far through life and caught each one of your tears in His bottle.⁸ The sufferer's tears are so important to God and He does not shy away from a good old-fashioned cry. Here's that tissue to blow your nose with.

There you go.

Feeling better?

Remember, don't get too indulgent with the sorrow of your wounding, as it's not good to stay in the ashes when God is asking you to rise because He knows you have a lot of flying to do in the next part of your journey. The enemy is quite content with you sitting in the relics and remains of your past because He knows that you're God's chosen instrument and He will try to keep that follow-up shot that is forming within you on the down low.

Sorry, I've gone off track. Where were we?

Ah yes, Pharaoh's daughter, the one who showed compassion to a crying Hebrew baby and changed the trajectory of his life forever. I'm so glad she wasn't entrenched in her father's cruel plan and was used by a good, good Father to pull off His perfect plan in raising a warrior. See what happens when we use a measured amount of compassion? It changes lives for the better and we don't get burned out in the process. The impossible becomes possible when we let God take the lead and let His compassion become the divine intervention for people's transformation. A song is rising, dear warrior, and it's time to start preparing that follow -up shot so the enemy knows your mean business. Read this aloud so he can hear it coming.

'I praise You, Eternal One.
You lifted me out of that deep, dark pit,
and denied my opponents the pleasure
of rubbing in their success.

Eternal One, my True God, I cried out to You for help;
You mended the shattered pieces of my life.
You lifted me from the grave with a mighty hand,
Gave me another chance,
And saved me from joining those in that dreadful pit.
Sing, all you who remain faithful!
Pour out your hearts to the Eternal with praise and melodies;
Let grateful music fill the air and bless His name."[9]
Psalm 30:1-4

Remember; weep if you must, dear warrior, then rise and lift your voice in song!

Prayer

Dear God,

Thank you for helping me along this journey and for giving me the strength and courage to stop looking back, as I trust in You with every step, and stick to the plan so I am able to rise up from the ashes of my past. Thank you for your compassion in the areas of my life where I can still feel the sting of abandonment or in the moments where I can feel left out because, if I'm honest, I still battle from time to time with my insecurities. When I choose to shrink back toward the safety of hiding, help me to rise up and move forward toward growth and become the courageous warrior You intended. Thank you for helping me see that even in the dark, hidden moments, You were developing my character in all the gaps and caves that I thought I'd get lost in. Teach me how to stay hidden *in* Christ, and camouflage me from the dangers so many wounded warriors often fall back into. You are love, and You guide and lead me through the trials and tests. Help me to not become too indulgent in mourning over what was, what could have been, and what will never come to pass, for You are a good, good Father who knows what is best for me. Amen.

Endnotes: Chapter Eight

Ref 1   Bevere, Lisa. 2020. *Godmothers: Why You Need One. How to Be One.* Grand Rapids, Mich.: Revell.

Ref 2   Exodus 2:5-6 Ecclesia Bible Society. 2012. *The Voice Bible: Step into the Story of Scripture.* Nashville: Thomas Nelson

Ref 3   Exodus 3:7-8 Ecclesia Bible Society. 2012. *The Voice Bible: Step into the Story of Scripture.* Nashville: Thomas Nelson

Ref 4   Brueggemann, Walter. 1997. *Theology of the Old Testament.* Augsburg Fortress MI.

Ref 5   Brody, Jessica. 2018. *Save the Cat! Writes a Novel : The Last Book on Novel Writing You'll Ever Need.* Berkeley, California: Ten Speed Press.

Ref 6   Wikipedia.org: Compassion Fatigue

Ref 7   Sister Miriam James Heidland 'Make all things new' YouTube watch

Ref 8   Psalm 56:8 Ecclesia Bible Society. 2012. *The Voice Bible: Step into the Story of Scripture.* Nashville: Thomas Nelson

Ref 9   Psalm 30:1-4 Ecclesia Bible Society. 2012. *The Voice Bible: Step into the Story of Scripture.* Nashville: Thomas Nelson

PART TWO

THE EXILE

CHAPTER NINE

Sealing the Deal

'The entire Old Testament is the story of God saying, "Trust me".' [1]
ANDY STANLEY

Well, my friend, you have crossed the first threshold of your journey to reigniting the warrior within! However, it is highly possible when you just read the words 'The Exile' you felt a slight tension, perhaps a pang of apprehension in choosing to commit yourself fully to the next dusty desert chapters. Don't worry, Miriam knows exactly why a warrior needs to spend some time going deep into the belly of the whale. All *you* need to do, dear warrior, is trust her leading.

Hmm, trust.

I know, it's so easy to say and even easier to break. It can be hard to trust when you've been wounded so badly. 'Once bitten twice shy' as the saying goes. Sometimes the bridge of trust that connects us in our relationships feels as solid as steel and you can skip along that thing without a care in the world because you know that person has got your back. Thinking back on some of our past relationships we realise it was a blend of neglect, compounded with a few disappointments, mixed with a variety of let-downs that rigged the bridge of trust up for detonation, finding ourselves stumbling around dazed and confused from the blast exposure because it all blew up in our face. And you can bet your last dollar, if the explosion didn't leave you with temporary deafness, then just for good measure, that slippery snake named Satan will keep on hissing his forked tongue into your ringing ears, reminding you how stupid you are because you haven't a clue what happened to you, do you? Well, if you're struggling to regroup and recall, he'll tell you quick smart that *you're* the problem. It's because God has indeed turned His back on you, left you, just like your friends. Even possibly *abandoned* you completely because of *your* failures and mistakes and that everything is undoubtably all *your* fault.

Really?

Oh yes, believe me, Satan is that cold-blooded.

This is the part where you need to remind your enemy, the one who loves to blood trail you through a forest of pain, that you *are* God's chosen instrument, and Miriam and I both know in full, painful detail how leadership can be a lonely road at times as some relationships, try as you might, feel more like a transaction rather than a connection. Listen, dear warrior, I think we've both learned in high school that not everyone is going to be your best buddy in this life, nor should they be either. But don't panic, it is here in the exile where you're going to gather all the materials to make and shake that follow-up shot so the enemy's poison-tipped arrows fly right past you. Miriam knows better than to skip the part that is known as 'The Exile' because every warrior needs to go through difficult transitions for a complete transformation. It is necessary—no *essential*, because the exile makes room for the warrior to turn aside from their past mistakes and look ahead toward a bright future, for it is in the fire of God's presence where true warriors are melded and shaped.

Feel His Heartbeat

Occasionally while I'm having my usual, personal worship session before I am ready to write, I take off my shoes (actually, my slippers), kneel before God and lift my hands heavenward. It's saying to God that I am on holy ground and I need His presence, His love, His comfort, and His guidance as I position myself down low at His feet. This posture of surrender is a reminder for me to seek His face always so I don't get caught up in all that yucky performance-based leadership again. Being a recovering people-pleaser, it's a real struggle at times to resist the perfectionist pull of making sure I say all the right things and do all the right things just so people like me. However, I've learned, if ever so slowly, to lean on God more and more in my leadership when I've felt like I've messed up because I've sensed I've done or said the wrong thing.

This is because I have come to realise that my deepest fear was that the trust bridge that connects me to God would inevitably blow up in my face because I didn't say everything right or do everything right. Trouble was, with all those booby traps and devices set up for detonation there was no room on that bridge for God's grace. That deep fear of being abandoned by Him was so branded across my fragile heart, so seared deep within my emotions, it had caused me to view my relationship with God in the same way as all my other past broken relationships. Do the right things, say the right things and God will love you was my secret mantra for years. What about you, dear warrior? Is this the drumming sound that your heartbeat marches to? I need you to know that doing all the right things and saying all the right things just so God loves you is a lie from the pit of hell, and if wounded warriors believe the fabrication that God will one day totally abandon us because of our failings, just like some of our relationships from our past, then I'm afraid to say that we don't really know God's heart at all.

A warrior understands battles are fought on their knees because 'when we get lower, we make room for God's answers'[2] comments Hanna E. Farwell, and it is in this low position of worship where God elevates His warriors so they can find the truth in all the confusion and chaos. 'So, bow down under God's strong hand; then when the time comes, God will lift you up. Since God cares for you, let Him carry all your burdens and worries.'[3] Hear that? *Let Him carry* all your burdens and worries. When we get on our knees and humble ourselves, we are making room for God's grace to answer all our doubts and worries. As far as this world is concerned, humility is deemed as a weakness or a deficiency rather than a virtue, however, humility is one of the warrior's greatest strengths because knowing who you are and *whose* you are raises the battle cry. But aren't warriors supposed to be full of confidence? Yes, but as Kris Vallotton states, 'Humility is not the absence of confidence... humility is a choice... the best way to choose humility is to choose to believe what God says about you. When we step out on the promises we have heard from our Father, we discover what is truly inside of us, and consequently, we are able to learn how to restrain our strength.'[4] Oh, I like that. Humility is restrained strength. Sounds like a warrior trait to me.

In the book of Ezekiel, the prophet sends a message of God's love to His people. Even though Jerusalem had been unfaithful, this was a message for them to repent and turn away from their idol worship, to humble themselves and turn back to God. This prophecy carried with it a promise of restoration and spiritual rebirth, a hope for God's chosen people.[5] 'When I passed by you again and looked upon you, indeed your time was the time of love; so, I spread My wing over you and covered your nakedness. Yes, I swore an oath to you and entered into a covenant with you and you became Mine... Then I washed you with water; yes, I thoroughly washed off your blood, and I anointed you with oil.'[6] God wants to re-establish you. He wants to settle your position. In fact, what He really wants is for you to feel His heartbeat, to enter into a covenant with Him as He bathes you in pure water and washes away the remnants of any clinging blood the blood trail of your wounding has left behind. God needs you to pay attention to the pulsation of His heart so you can distinguish the truth from the enemy's falsehoods. He needs you to know who you are, dear warrior, because when you've been running out of fear of abandonment it can cause you to lose yourself in the desert. Just ask Miriam about her baby brother, Moses.

The D.I.Y. Shot

When studying the leadership of Miriam, we must include her brother, Moses. Not just because he was commissioned by God to lead His people out of slavery and into their freedom, but because with God's help, Moses learned to become a warrior by rising up out of the ashes of his past.

We find Moses stumbling around dazed and confused in the desert sands from the blast exposure of a relationship blowing up in his face. The trust bridge had been broken between himself and Pharaoh, developing a chasm so wide that Moses fell into it from a great height. A fall that found him going from a delightful, desired son taken from the waters of the Nile to now a dishevelled delinquent forced into exile. All because Moses decided to take matters into his own hands and fire a makeshift follow-up shot straight from the hip, one that was forged from the fires of repayment rather than revival. 'He saw an Egyptian beating a Hebrew, one of his own people. Glancing this way and that and seeing no one, he killed the Egyptian and hid him in the sand.'[7]

Moses thought no one had seen this unceremonious burial of the Egyptian.

But someone had.

And when Pharaoh got an earful of Moses' do-it-yourself follow-up shot, he wasn't happy. 'When Pharaoh heard of this, he tried to kill Moses, but Moses fled from Pharaoh and went to live in Midian.'[7] Moses spent the next forty years running from the ghost of that unnamed Egyptian. Forty years in hiding because he took matters into his own hands. He thought he'd left that body of evidence entombed deep within Egypt's sands but the sound from his faulty follow-up shot had rung out from the ground up and Pharaoh wanted Moses dead too. The eerie sounds from his past had rung in Moses' ears for forty long years and haunted him ever since. You could say that the shadows from his past spooked him out of his destiny.

Now he found himself in the deafening silence of exile.

You see, the thing about D.I.Y. follow-up shots is that the slapdash, shoddy workmanship of the shot causes it to miss the mark every time. As we wounded warriors start to feel that all too familiar feeling of abandonment, it causes us to not fully trust God with His promises. Our emotions get us a little antsy and we end up rolling up our sleeves and saying to God, 'I'll take my destiny from here, just in case you're deciding to abandon me.' This is where our D.I.Y. follow-up shot may *sound* right to us and everyone else within ear shot, but let me warn you, dear warrior, it ain't gonna fly. Taking matters into our own hands and creating handmade shots instead of waiting patiently for the carefully crafted God-made follow-up shot to form is what the enemy loves because he's not rattled by our makeshift rubber bullets for he knows they have no firepower. Before the craft glue has even has chance to dry on our follow-up shot the enemy knows that it's all made up by our own undoing and will never reach its target. This is because D.I.Y. shots are always aimed at the wrong thing. And no matter how skilfully you've tried to cover up and bury your own way of doing things, God knows, and He will lead you into exile so your wilderness experience will knock some sense into you.

The shame we feel from something not working out or the grief we feel from a relationship failure is because we got scared and took matters into our own hands instead of fully trusting God with the plan. Shame always leads us along the path of disappointment which leads to grief and then grief leads us to those recognisable feelings of abandonment. The enemy will happily hand you craft supplies, so you're kept busy making as many makeshift follow-up shots as you like, and this is all the ammunition he needs to berate and belittle you into hiding.

Commissioned by a Fiery Blaze

How was God going to dimmish that deep fear of abandonment Moses had possibly felt for the past forty years and show him that he was indeed His chosen warrior? How could God guide Moses out of the shadows of painful regrets and away from the desert plains, leading him under the shadow of the Almighty, gently guiding him out of hiding so he could learn to hide in the covering of God's feathers and find protection under His great wings? (Psalm 91:1-4) That deep set fear of abandonment had to go so that Moses could fully trust God with his future.

I think we can put Bible giants, like Moses, on pedestals and believe that they never went through all the same emotions we feel because of their great success. But Moses wrestled with his failure, his deep fear of abandonment and his regretful behaviour of burying the unnamed Egyptian under the sand. Sure, Moses became a warrior, but believe it or not, he was human just like the rest of us. Don't you find the word *warrior* conjures up all sorts of images in our minds, like champion, fighter, and hero. However, you get the feeling these flat and flaky 2D images can represent a distorted picture of what a real warrior looks like. Caricature warriors have no depth and are not much use in battles because they're all show and no substance. Real warriors, genuine 3D warriors, face challenges head on but they still feel all kinds of deep emotions and must tussle and scuffle with them at times, however, this helps them in their growth and development. Brené Brown suggests that failure teaches us the value found in our regrets because it's a strong emotional reminder that we need to change and grow.[8] The burning bush in the desert was where God commissioned Moses to change and to grow, to leave his past behind so he could move forward into his destiny. In Exodus 3:3 Moses said, 'I will now turn aside and see this great sight, why the bush does not burn.'[9] Why would the Bible be so specific with this detail? Why not just say, 'Moses saw a bush burning'. I believe the turning aside to look at the fiery flames was Moses coming alongside, to partner with God as it's the next verse that seals the deal. 'So, when the Lord saw that he turned aside to look, God called to him from the midst of the bush and said, "Moses! Moses!"'[9] When the Lord *saw that he turned aside.* God knew Moses was ready for his commissioning. Moses was willing to come alongside God, to partner with Him and turn from his past so he could step into his future. The heat from the burning bush melted the wax on the covenant and secured the verification stamp of approval from God, as the fire of His presence made sure the deal was sealed.

The flames burned up any doubt Moses felt about his calling and shifted the focus off himself and onto others. I believe the burning bush was a defining, intimate God moment for Moses that he carried through all the ten plagues and the miracle moments toward the Promised Land as God showed up for His people time and time again. The fire in the burning bush not only burnt up all the feelings of doubt but the deep fear of abandonment, giving Moses a hope to cling onto. Yahweh was revealing that his forty-year exile was nearing its expiry date and sealed the deal on Moses' future by melting His waxed kingdom crest into his calling with the fire of His presence, verifying and validating the Sender's identity. When Moses asked, 'Why is this bush not burning up? I need to move a little closer to get a better look'[10] this was the spark that ignited the warrior within him. 'Don't come any closer. Take of your sandals and stand barefoot on the ground of My presence, for this ground is holy ground.'[10] A shoeless Moses had entered into God's presence like a barefoot priest in the temple as his dusty sandals that were covered with forty years of impurities of all sorts were set aside for this sacred moment.[11]

Listen in, dear warrior, can you hear God's voice in the flames of His presence? Take of your shoes as this is holy ground. This is a sacred moment. I AM is sending you. And that promise is as good as the One who speaks it. Barefoot believer, are you ready to step into your destiny? *What? Me?* Even in my hiding, my doubts, and my failures, God *still* calls me. You'd better believe it, and no lies from the forked tongue of the enemy are going to stop God's outrageous, extravagant over the top love for you. It's a fact. Your warrior contract is stamped with God's kingdom approval and is signed, sealed, and delivered to you by the fiery flames of His presence. The One who will never abandon you even in the backside of the desert. Because He is the One who believes you are still precious enough to be found.

Endnotes: Chapter Nine

Ref 1   Stanley, Andy. 2012. *Deep & Wide: Creating Churches Unchurched People Love To Attend.* By Andy Stanley. Zondervan. Grand Rapids. Michigan.

Ref 2   Farwell, Hanna. 2010. *The Sword and the Tamborine: Becoming a Warrior Through Worship.* Destiny Image Publishers.

Ref 3   1 Peter 5:6-7 Ecclesia Bible Society. 2012. *The Voice Bible: Step into the Story of Scripture.* Nashville: Thomas Nelson

Ref 4   Johnson, Beni, Bill Johnson, Danny Silk, Kris Vallotton, Kevin Dedmon, and Banning Liebscher. 2010. *Spiritual Java.* Destiny Image Publishers.

Ref 5   Biblical Commentary. *Spiritual Warfare Bible.* 2012. Lake Mary, Florida, Charisma House.

Ref 6   Ezekiel 16:8-9 *Spiritual Warfare Bible.* 2012. Lake Mary, Florida, Charisma House.

Ref 7   Exodus 2:11 -15 Syswerda, Jean, and Faith Organization.2001. NIV Women of Faith Study Bible: New International Version. Grand Rapids, Mich.: Zondervan.

Ref 8   Brown, Brené. 2017. *Rising Strong: If We Are Brave Enough, Often Enough, We Will Fall. This Is A Book About Getting Back Up.* Vermilion. Imprint Of Ebury Publishing. Penguin Random House, UK.

Ref 9   Exodus 3:3-4 *Spiritual Warfare Bible.* 2012. Lake Mary, Florida, Charisma House.

Ref 10   Exodus 3:3 -5 Ecclesia Bible Society. 2012. *The Voice Bible: Step into the Story of Scripture.* Nashville: Thomas Nelson

Ref 11   Walton, John H, Victor Harold Matthews, and Mark William Chavalas. 2000.*The IVP Bible Background Commentary Old Testament.* Downers Grove, Ill. Intervarsity Press.

CHAPTER TEN

The Deliverer Delivers

> *'Faith isn't a noun; faith is a verb...*
> *a journeying with no map but God alone.*
> *Faith is not being sure which way,*
> *but going always toward Him, in Him.'* [1]
> ANN VOSKAMP

Remember way back in chapter three I promised that I wanted to spend a little more time on the fear of God and how it helps the warrior to rise up? Well, now that we're further and deeper into our journey, a promise is a promise, and seeing as we're about to embark into exile territory and already we're quickly moving forward into chapter ten, I think here is as good as spot as any to take a break, set up the camping chairs and start another fire, one that's going to warm up those packets of soup so we can all drink in some wisdom of how our brave leader, Miriam is finally reunited with her baby brother after many years, and why leaving the desert required a holy reverent fear of Yahweh so Moses could trust in the promise that God would indeed send a barrage of follow-up shots to rescue His people from Pharaoh's rule.

I know you've patiently waited through a fair few chapters for the promise I gave to you about the fear of God and how it helps a warrior to rise up, however, God's promises can feel even more painstakingly slow when you're eager for a breakthrough in your circumstances. And as the energy from the campfire slowly heats up our food, I do hope, dear warrior, there is an energy heating up within you, a song rising that echoes the sound of heaven. Nevertheless, you're probably feeling we're wasting time just sitting around a campfire, listening to Miriam's story of escape from the slave-master Pharaoh, while sipping hot soup when we should be fighting battles and firing our follow-up shots at the enemy. This is one of the reasons why I asked Miriam to lead our warrior expedition, as the Israelites desperately wanted to rise up out of the slavery of Egypt and move into the freedom of the Promised Land. And yet, they would have to learn a few God-fearing lessons in the exile of the wilderness before they were truly ready to enter into the land God promised them. Don't be in such a hurry, Miriam will get to that incredible part of her story soon, leaving you slack-jawed and on the edge of your camping chair as she spins a tale of what happened through each of the ten plagues in Egypt until Pharaoh was finally depleted enough to release the Israelites from under his slave-driver hand. Miriam knows the techniques of God and how He shapes an effective, authentic follow-up shot so it lands on its target, and you'll be interested to note that it isn't necessarily in the planning. The real key to bringing Pharaoh's who believe they are gods to their knees is all in the preparation. We can't afford to squander our follow-up shots by closing our eyes and hoping for the best as we randomly fire at our enemy, as those shots are not going to follow-through. Preparation helps a warrior to strategically fight in the battles ahead. Perhaps we should glean a little wisdom from Abraham Lincoln as he affirmed the fundamental importance of doing the groundwork of preparation over planning. 'If I had eight hours to chop down a tree, I'd spend the first six hours sharpening my axe.'[2] Old Abe had done his preparation homework.

Strongholds are what Satan uses to warrant barriers in our lives, but a wise warrior understands a good foothold is what steadies our aim. Abiding in God's presence is paramount to warriors so we can confidently fire our follow-up shot back at the enemy. Interestingly, another word for footing is resting place[3] and when we rest in God and abide in Him, that's all the support we need. Wasteful shots are a waste of a warrior's time and the enemy's reply will not be so haphazard. We need to stay as sharp as Lincoln's axe as our enemy is rising up too and he is gathering his army whose methodical, meticulous, careful approach is as efficient as Pharaoh's army. We must be just as disciplined and orderly as our enemy, otherwise our follow-up shot will be lost in the thicket and its inefficiency will come at a great cost. We need to trust in God's timing as He trains and equips His warriors, knowing that the Deliverer will deliver us.

Whom Do You Fear?

Think back to that burning bush moment where God commissioned Moses for a second while you gaze into the flames of the campfire. When God told him that He'd heard the cry of His people and He had seen their misery because of the Egyptian slavedrivers, God shared the blueprints of His battle plan with

Moses. Regardless of how many '*I will be with you*' statements God said to Moses, his response seemed to lean more on the fear of man rather than the fear of God. Moses started out well with his reply of, 'Here I am'.[4] (Exodus 3:4) All the same, once the sentence, 'I am sending you to Pharaoh to bring my people the Israelites out of Egypt'[4] (Exodus 3:10) left God's mouth, Moses suddenly did a back flip on his responses and started finding excuses as to why God had chosen the wrong guy. 'But who am I, that I should go to Pharaoh and bring the Israelites out of Egypt?'[4] (Exodus 3:11) 'Suppose I go to the Israelites and say to them, "The God of your fathers has sent me to you..."'[4] (Exodus 3:13) 'What if they do not believe me or listen to me and say, "The Lord did not appear to you?"' [4] (Exodus 4:1) 'O Lord, I have never been eloquent, neither in the past nor since you have spoken to your servant. I am slow of speech and tongue.' [4] (Exodus 4:10) 'O Lord, please send someone else to do it.' [4] (Exodus 4:13)

It seems Moses was taking the scissors to his fresh pair of wings and clipping away the flight feathers that would send him to back to Egypt. Instead of soaring up from the flames and experiencing a Phoenix rebirthing, his insecurities sent him spiralling back down into the ashes. He needed more time, more planning. Good grief, he wasn't just going to... *wing it!*

See how the fear of man gets in the way of what God has called His warriors to do. Why is the fear of man so debilitating to a warrior? If we're ensnared by the fear of man then we will 'live on the run, hiding from harm or reproach, constantly avoiding rejection and confrontation'[5] as John Bevere disclosed in his brilliant book, *The Fear of the Lord*. He goes on to say that the fear of God means we reverence Him, give Him all the honour, and praise He deserves.[5] A holy fear of God is very different from running away as a result of fearing man. Living on the run so we avoid rejection, hiding out of fear because confronting people means that we could be left abandoned once again isn't where God wants us to be. Been there. Done that. Considering the task that lay ahead for Moses we shouldn't be so hard on him, as I feel his reaction does sound very familiar. It certainly does to me because I've spent a lot of years in leadership and found that each time my fear of man trumped my fear of God things never really turned out that well. I too went from 'Here I am' to 'Send someone else' rather quickly when I found out what God was asking of me. This is why the fear of the Lord is so crucial to a wounded warrior. We will never serve God fully and trust His promises for our lives completely when our hearts are set on self-preservation due to our fear of man. Proverbs 29:25 says, 'The fear of man brings a snare, but whoever trusts in *and* puts his confidence in the Lord will be exalted and safe.'[6]

Reunion

'Now the Lord had said to Moses in Midian, "Go back to Egypt, for all the men who wanted to kill you are dead."' As things go, this was at least a small comfort to our worried warrior. 'So, Moses took his wife and his sons, put them on a donkey and started back to Egypt. And he took his staff of God in his hand.'[7] Imagine Miriam and Aaron seeing their baby brother after forty years of being separated? I don't know what it's like to have a blood brother as my two brothers are through marriage, but I do have a sister I haven't seen for about nine years. She lives in England and we were planning a family trip back in 2020, but one word stopped those plans. Pandemic. And no amount of preparation or planning saw that one coming! Recently, my brother and sister-in-law flew over to Australia for a holiday, now that international travel restrictions have been lifted. While we were nervously waiting for them to come through customs at the airport, I watched other families kiss and embrace one another because they hadn't seen each other for so long. It was so lovely to watch. Now, my brother-in-law isn't well known for being overly sentimental, so I wasn't expecting any spontaneous affection in his greeting to us. But in spite of my doubts, I was surprised to discover that four years apart from your family can change even the most stiff, English upper lip, for when my brother and sister-in-law finally did come through the double doors and down the exit ramp he was already crying! Apparently, he had been crying on and off throughout the long flight over from England. The best part was that as he ran to greet my husband, his big brother, and embrace him with a huge bear hug that lasted minutes, I could only stand in appreciation of what family truly means.

It was a beautiful thing.

Miriam's teary eyes reflecting in the camp fire's glow as she sips on her soup reveal how special family reunions are. The Bible doesn't expand on the moment Miriam and Aaron embrace Moses after forty years of being apart. Be that as it may, I can't help but imagine it would've been something special to see. All those thoughts of wondering if their brother was still alive or if he'd died long ago in the back of beyond must have disappeared into thin air as she possibly hung onto his every word of his amazing experience in the desert and how God told him, through a burning bush, to come back to Egypt so he could lead God's people out of slavery.

Over a period of time, Miriam's edge in leadership could have dulled slightly during those forty years as she went about her business. Her effectiveness was possibly out of alignment and she needed to be sharpened once again by a red-hot testimony of how the fire of God's presence reignited the warrior within her baby brother.[8] Now, with Moses back in Egypt, their family reunion was up against some serious resistance with the new Pharaoh in town.[8] This sheriff wasn't prepared to give up his badge of authority and let God's people go *that* easily. Regardless of Pharaoh's stubborn response, one by one each plague God sent was like rapid-fire follow-up shots coming from a sniper rifle straight at the Egyptians, letting Pharaoh know who oversaw, Operation, Let My People Go!

What I love about God's sovereignty is that none of Pharaoh's nonsense frustrated His divine plan to rescue and redeem the Israelites out of their oppression. With the plagues now in full swing, the leadership extraction team of Moses, Miriam, and Aaron sharpened and ready, and God's people 'dressed and ready to go at a moment's notice—with sandals on your feet and a walking stick in your hand'[9] it was now time for the tenth plague to deliver the final death blow to Pharaoh's deity.

Restored

When Pharaoh discovered the limp body of his first-born son in the middle of the night, he sent for Moses and Aaron. 'Get up, get out from among my people, both you and the Israelites and go serve the Lord, as you said.'[10] After years of oppression and being stripped of everything, including their dignity, the Israelites were finally free from the tyranny of Pharaoh's rule. Imagine if Moses had allowed his fear of man to gain the upper hand from his fear of God? As Barbara Wentroble clearly states, 'Fear. If we let it, will wrap its ugly tentacles around us and choke out the very life that God breathed into us.'[11] The ignition that started a fire in Moses' warrior veins from his burning bush moment in God's presence was slowly being snuffed out by the fear he felt from his insecurities as its tentacles wrapped around his heart like a giant octopus. 'Until we break off the fear of man we will never rise up into our destiny.'[11] So true, Barbara. The fear of God will help us to restore everything that the enemy pilfered from us. When we choose to fear God over man then our follow-up shot will sound like this, 'It was like a dream come true when you freed us from our bondage and brought us back to Zion! We laughed and laughed and overflowed with gladness. We were left shouting for joy and singing your praise… now, Lord, do it again! Restore us to our former glory!'[12] (Psalm 126:1-2) God will bring back, build up and re-establish you when you depend upon Him to transform you from, worried about what others think, to a warrior whose follow-up shots are coated in the fear of the Lord. After all, this fear is one to be kept, for it is where true wisdom is birthed and found.[13]

Abide

While we're sharing campfire stories, I just want to take a moment to speak about abiding in God. Recognising when we're running out of a fear of man instead of running to God in holy reverence and fear for Him is where we can listen to the wrong voices. Satan cranks up his sound system as he starts to put a spin on his typical golden oldie lies, a classic way to get warriors to turn into worriers leaving them dancing to his tune like puppets on a string. God needed to take Moses out of the desert and relocate him back into Egypt, and his 'turning aside I need to abide' burning bush moment was the refining fire that ignited a warrior within. Sometimes God needs to shake things up a little else we'll stay in the ashes forever. He has to burn off the things that have to go so our heart burns for Him.

Abiding does that.

For 'we can't do the works of Christ by human might or earthly power; we can only do them with the heart of Christ' [14] suggests Beth Moore. I can put my hand on my heart and solemnly swear Moses could never have rescued all those Israelites in his own strength. Remember, he tried that with the unnamed Egyptian, and his D.I.Y. shot sent him running into the desert. He needed God's strength to get the job done.

Let me ask you, dear warrior, doesn't your heart yearn for something more, something greater than where you currently are in your faith? God chose you for a purpose and He wants His full presence in your day-to-day life. Don't listen to the lies of the enemy reminding you that you're not good enough to do amazing things for God. God says that you're worth finding and He wants you to abide in Him. He wants you to know that there is no risk of failure in Him. Don't believe me? Okay, I'll just let you read Psalm 62 for yourself then.

'I stand silently to listen for the one I love,
Waiting as long as it takes for the Lord to rescue me.
For God alone has become my Saviour.
He alone is my safe place;
His wrap-around presence always protects me.
For he is my champion defender;

there's no risk of failure with God.
So why would I let worry paralyse me,
Even when troubles multiply around me?"[15]

Did you hear that melody? That love celebration to the Pure Shining One?[16] A song is rising as we *listen* for the one we love and when we chose to abide in God we are giving Him our full attention. To fear God instead of fearing man shifts the focus off ourselves and gives Satan no bargaining chip to negotiate or manipulate us with. Abiding with God, just like Moses did at the burning bush, means that we have chosen to turn aside from our past and move forward into God's presence because faith is the substance of things we hoped for, the evidence of things not seen.[17]

Endnotes: Chapter Ten

Ref 1   Voskamp, Ann. 2022. *Waymaker: Finding the Way to the Life You've Always Dreamed Of.* Nashville, Tennessee: W Publishing Group, An Imprint Of Thomas Nelson.

Ref 2   Matthews, Tom. LinkedIn Blog Post. 'The Importance of preparation—sharpen the axe!' Published 21st Jan 2020.

Ref 3   thesaurus.com 'footing'

Ref 4   (Exodus 3:4) (Exodus 3:10) (Exodus 3:11) (Exodus 3:13) (Exodus 4:1) (Exodus 4:13) Syswerda, Jean, and Faith Organization.2001. NIV Women of Faith Study Bible: New International Version. Grand Rapids, Mich.: Zondervan.

Ref 5   Bevere, John 1997. *The Fear of the Lord.* Charisma House Publishing.

Ref 6   Proverbs 29:25 *Amplified Holy Compact Bible: Captures the Full Meaning behind the Original Greek and Hebrew.* 2015. Grand Rapids, Michigan: Zondervan.

Ref 7   Exodus 4:19-20 Syswerda, Jean, and Faith Organization.2001. NIV Women of Faith Study Bible: New International Version. Grand Rapids, Mich.: Zondervan.

Ref 8   Kunneman, Brenda. 2010. *Decoding Hell's Propaganda.* Destiny Image Publishers INC.

Ref 9   Exodus 12:11 Ecclesia Bible Society. 2012. *The Voice Bible: Step into the Story of Scripture.* Nashville: Thomas Nelson

Ref 10   Exodus 12:31 *Amplified Holy Compact Bible: Captures the Full Meaning behind the Original Greek and Hebrew.* 2015. Grand Rapids, Michigan: Zondervan.

Ref 11   Wentroble, Barbara. 2006. *Rise to your Destiny, Woman of God.* Gospel Light Publications.

Ref 12   Psalm 126:1-2 The Passion Translation: New Testament with Psalms, Proverbs, and Song of Songs, Second Edition. Passion & Fire Ministries, Inc. Broadstreet Publishing: 2018.

Ref 13   Psalm 111:10 The Passion Translation: New Testament with Psalms, Proverbs, and Song of Songs, Second Edition. Passion & Fire Ministries, Inc. Broadstreet Publishing: 2018.

Ref 14   Moore, Beth. 2020. *Chasing Vines: Finding Your Way to an Immensely Fruitful Life.* Carol Stream, Illinois: Tyndale Momentum, The Tyndale Nonfiction Imprint.

Ref 15   Psalm 62:1-2 The Passion Translation: New Testament with Psalms, Proverbs, and Song of Songs, Second Edition. Passion & Fire Ministries, Inc. Broadstreet Publishing: 2018.

Ref 16 'The Inscription' Commentary of Psalm 62. The Passion Translation: New Testament with Psalms, Proverbs, and Song of Songs, Second Edition. Passion & Fire Ministries, Inc. Broadstreet Publishing: 2018.

Ref 17 Hebrews 11:1 *Spiritual Warfare Bible. 2012. Lake Mary, Florida, Charisma House.*

CHAPTER ELEVEN

A Dry Road

'Whatever story you're telling, it will be more interesting if, at the end you add, "... and then everything burst into flames".' [1]
BRIAN P. CLEARY

Okay, lean in, I have something to tell you about our courageous leader, Miriam, as she pours water on the campfire while we're packing up the soup bowls and deciding who's turn it is to carry the backpack. When studying Miriam, I discovered that water is the theme that runs right through her life and has played a significant part in each pivotal moment of her story. The reason why I'm sharing this with you now is because when Miriam shows you the map in just a moment and runs her finger along the route of the next leg of our journey, you're going to notice there is a much shorter road that will lead us to the same point far quicker. A word of caution here, dear warrior, just in case you feel a wildfire of unholy words rising up on the inside of you when you realise this longer route Miriam is leading you toward will add a lot of extra miles onto the journey. A lot. Nevertheless, it's not Miriam you need to pick a fight with, it's God, as lengthy roads are a speciality of His. And He will, if needed, direct would-be warriors into long, drawn-out journeys for reasons God only knows.

We left the Exodus story at the point where Pharaoh had finally relented to Moses and let God's people go. The Egyptians, after all the drama of the ten plagues, were now ready to see the back of Yahweh's troublemakers and advised the Israelites to get out of dodge as quickly as possible. But in all the hast this meant the bread the Israelites were preparing had no time to rise. 'The Egyptians urged the people to hurry and leave the country. "For otherwise," they said, "we will all die!" So, the people took their dough before the yeast was added and carried it on their shoulders in kneading troughs wrapped in clothing... with the dough they had brought from Egypt, they baked cakes of unleavened bread. The dough was without yeast because they had been driven out of Egypt and did not have time to prepare food for themselves.'[2] (Exodus 12:33-39) This is why generations after the Exodus event celebrated the Passover meal with unleavened bread[3] as yeast needs time for dough to rise. The apostle Paul mentions yeast in 1 Corinthians 5:6-8 as he brings in some pastoral correction to the community of believers. 'Your flip and callous arrogance in these things bothers me. You pass it off as a small thing, but it's anything but that. Yeast, too, is a "small thing", but it works its way through the whole batch of bread dough pretty fast. So, get rid of this "yeast". Our true identity is flat and plain, not puffed up with the wrong kind of ingredient. The Messiah, our Passover Lamb, has already been sacrificed for the Passover meal, and we are the unraised part of the feast. So, let's live out our part in the Feast, not as raised bread swollen with yeast of evil, but as flat bread—simple, genuine, unpretentious.'[4] Why is Paul talking about the Exodus to New Testament believers? Well, when you read Paul's two letters to the Corinthians you can almost hear the exasperation in his voice. He's like a teacher whose students just don't get the lessons being taught them no matter how many times, how many different ways, or how many angles he approaches things. The trouble Paul was dealing with was that the Corinthians' mindset was so steeped in the culture that surrounded them they didn't seem too fazed by the 'small' scandal of sexual immorality within their Christian community. However, Paul loved them too much to turn a blind eye to the sin the Corinthians were trying to gloss over and cover up. Paul's confronting correction was not so he could lord the gospel over them, waving his pointing finger and telling them how terrible they were, it was for the care and protection of the whole community.

Looking back on my own leadership journey, I wished I hadn't had allowed my fear of what people would think of me override the need to bring correction to someone who thought covering up a little sin would be more helpful to the church. Paul is so right, for yeast is such a small thing, but my oh my, it certainly works its way through the whole batch of dough quickly. If you've ever baked bread, you'll know that it only takes a very small amount of yeast for dough to rise, and as warriors rising, it only takes a little arrogance, a little hidden sin for us to become swollen with pride and what rises isn't for the glory of God. Flat bread, as Paul states, is simple, genuine, and unpretentious as it has no time for yeast to do its work.

Wandering

Now, before you feel the need to air your views about yeast to your neighbours, tact and wisdom are needed, for we are not called to bring correction to the world, but we do have a responsibility to develop and help believers within the church. Discipline, if done correctly, can save an awful lot of heartache and pain as correction should always point people back to the redemption of God's saving grace.[5] Sin should bother us, as it did Paul, and interestingly yeast was often used in Scripture as a symbol for sin.[6] As I've mentioned, lengthy roads are a speciality of Gods and when we're footloose and fancy-free in our faith because we've become too puffed up with the wrong kind of ingredient, God will press, shape, squeeze, and form us into warriors who fear Him, as this is what gets activated and not the sin we want to keep hidden. Don't be surprised when your ego becomes bloated and boastful, just like the Corinthians because this is the exact moment God takes out His heavenly measuring tape and marks out a strip of road that's just about the right length to stop your faith from wandering. Unleavened bread in the Passover celebrations was a reminder to God's people that He looks for simple, genuine, unpretentious faith. The sad truth is that many think small sins are not as dangerous as big sins and our wandering, if not corrected, turns into a faith behaviour and we can end up living a lifestyle that never settles anything with God. But sin is sin as far as God is concerned and habits look great on nuns but bad habits, if left to their own devices, can start sizing up bits of timber that end up framing a mind. A wooden framed viewpoint has some disadvantages and one of them is temperature extremes,[7] for it's the humidity not humility that causes a stubborn mind to sweat as it can't see the wood for the trees. Another word for yeast is pest,[8] and pest infestations are another disadvantage to wooden thinking, as a plank in your eye can attract many a bug. If we continue to ignore the plank, you can be sure by the time we've rummaged through our handbags looking for a pair of tweezers in an attempt to help out a fellow Christian's annoying speck in their own eye, an invasion of termites would have eaten their way through the framework of your faith until there are more holes in your theology than a block of Swiss cheese.

The Wilderness Way

You may feel this chapter has hit you like a two-by-four, but believe me, I want you to rise well, dear warrior, with the right motives. When we read about the Phoenix rising out of the ashes it's the best part of the story, however, the firebird's deep transformation takes shape when it's in the ashes. Change can be a slow process at times and feel long-winded and tedious as God leads you into the wilderness way. And yet, it's in the dehydrated, ash-pit parts of your precious scarred soul that a fountain springs forth with the promise of a fresh, new beginning. The Israelites had truly been brought up out of Egypt by God's mighty hand,[9] however, God wasn't done with His lessons in showing His people how to step out in complete faith and trust Him with their future. 'When Pharaoh let the people go, God did not lead them on the road through the Philistine country, though that was shorter. For God said, "If they face war, they might change their minds and return to Egypt." So, God led the people around by the desert road toward the Red Sea.'[10] The shorter route was through Philistine territory and was heavily defended for it was used by armies and trade caravans.¹¹ Looking at the map, the shorter route makes perfect sense to us, right? That may be so, but God knew that His people were not an army who was equipped to fight, not in this part of their story anyway. They were a rabble of ex-slaves who were only just discovering their flight feathers for the first time in hundreds of years, and this is why God needed them to travel down a long, dry road to gain enough momentum so they could catch the updraft and rise from the ashes as warriors.

I need you to pay attention to what I'm about to say, for it is this critical part in our transformation where the enemy studies the blueprints of his carefully laid plan. He can never stop what God has spoken over us, but he can slow our calling right down to a grinding halt until we're taxiing around in circles on the asphalt because we're too scared to try out our new wings. Second thoughts, a flip-flop mindset, and backpedalling doubts about God's promises over our lives activates the law surrounding the enemy's *change your mind* policy like fine print on a receipt. He is after all, legalistic, and this loophole is where the devil's devious schemes take shape. God knew if the Israelites took the shortcut and faced the military, well-oiled machine of the Philistine soldiers, then they'd be back in Egypt making bricks quicker than you could say the word 'pyramid'.

Think about your own life. What dry road has God sent you down? Does it feel like it goes on and on forever? We warriors can get bored and thirst for more action in our stories because the aridness of the experience feels like God has gone off script. And yet, it is the wilderness way where we learn to recognise the pillar of cloud by day and the pillar of fire by night that is the presence of God that goes before us and is always with us as we travel along dry roads. It says in Hebrews 11:27 'By faith he left

Egypt, not fearing the king's anger; he persevered because he saw him who is invisible.'[12] The wilderness way helps warriors to see what was once invisible become visible and when that happens our perspective changes. The adjustment in our development feels like the slowest part of our journey but it helps in the longevity of our transformation. Warriors are no flash in the pan and God builds things to last. As T.D. Jakes suggests, 'Anything that is made well is made slow. The quality must go in before His name goes on it.' [13] Quality is the trait of a warrior and it is the dry road conditions where the Maker's mark is revealed, letting the enemy know he's found the genuine article.

Fire and Water

Perhaps I'm overthinking this part of the Exodus story, but I was chatting with my friend about the way God led His people along the wilderness way and we concluded that God's presence was through a pillar of cloud and fire which harmonized Miriam's life theme of water and Moses' commissioning in the burning bush. Although we could be theologically way off course, it's at least something to ponder. But regardless of how unproductive those thoughts may be, one thing is certain, the pillar provided guidance through the dry road. When we realise that God is in no hurry in our transformation, we can relax a little. For in His infinite wisdom, I believe, this part of the story reminds us that even in our wilderness moments God is *still* present, He *still* covers us, and He *still* leads us through. All the Israelites needed to do was to trust and follow God because as I've already mentioned, obedience is the way. And as simplistic as that seems, it's the way of the warrior. For the wilderness has a way of tuning out all the things that once pushed you down, caused you to shrink back, to doubt, and to hesitate so you're able to move forward with confidence and find a song in your heart, knowing deep down in your soul that God is leading you onwards and upwards and He won't let you go.

Flight to Plight

When the enemy realises, you're deadly serious about all this warrior business and you've gained enough courage to test out your wings as you slowly rise up from the ashes, the flight from slavery to freedom can rapidly turn into a plight of predicament as you suddenly find yourself between a rock and a hard place. The rising conflict between Pharaoh and Moses seemed to have dissipated as the king of Egypt had indeed relented in letting God's people go. All the same, God wants to make known that He is the One who helps His people get through a crisis and brings a resolution to our problems.

In chapter fourteen of the Exodus story this is the part when the action starts to ignite again. 'When the king of Egypt was told that the people were gone, he and his servants changed their minds. They said, "What have we done, letting Israel, our slave labour, go free?" So, he had his chariots harnessed up and got his army together... God made Pharaoh king of Egypt stubborn, determined to chase the Israelites as they walked out on him without even looking back.'[14] (Exodus 14:3-7) Just remember, dear warrior, when you walk out on something that has ruled over you all your life and you do it without even giving it a backward glance, then watch out, that thing is used to being in control and isn't quite ready for your exodus. Whether it's withdrawing from striving, people-pleasing, perfectionism, never feeling good enough, abandonment issues, or an addiction you've been a slave to for many years, please, for the love of all God's promises, just keep walking toward your freedom and don't look back at Egypt.

While listening to Miriam retell the Exodus story, I can sense you've been wanting to ask her many questions as we've travelled along this wilderness, dry road. She asks you what you want to know, so you've decided you'll go for the most pressing question as it's been bugging you for a while. 'Why did God make Pharaoh stubborn and determined to chase after the Israelites when he'd let them go? And since we're on the subject, why did God go to all the trouble and misery of the ten plagues to cause Pharaoh to relent when He was only going to make him more dog-determined to capture God's people again? Why did the Phoenix flight out of Egypt only to end up in a plight with Pharaoh and his army chasing after them? I don't understand all this because Wendy said that changing our minds is a bad thing, but it was God Himself that changed Pharaoh's mind! This makes no sense.'

And breathe.

The glint in Miriam's eye does not go unnoticed as she chuckles softly to herself while gazing heavenward. The pause as you wait for her reply feels just as long as the dry road we've been travelling along. Come on, Miriam, it's getting to the point of being awkward. Eventually she clears her throat and utters six words in reply to your long way round, wilderness way, dry road questions. Although short, Miriam's answer is packed with as much explosive power as a stick of dynamite. Pointing heavenward she replies:

'So, He gets all the glory.'

Endnotes: Chapter Eleven

Ref 1   Cleary, Brian P. Quote. Website: goodreads.com

Ref 2   Exodus 12:33-39. Syswerda, Jean, and Faith Organization.2001. NIV Women of Faith Study Bible: New International Version. Grand Rapids, Mich.: Zondervan.

Ref 3   Keener, Craig S. 1993. *The IVP Bible Background Commentary New Testament.* Downers Grove. Ill. InterVarsity Press.

Ref 4   1 Corinthians 5:6-8. Peterson, Eugene H. 1995. *The Message Bible.* Colorado Springs, Co: Navpress.

Ref 5   Biblical Commentary of 1 Corinthians 5:6-8. Ecclesia Bible Society. 2012. *The Voice Bible: Step into the Story of Scripture.* Nashville: Thomas Nelson

Ref 6   Commentary on page 107 of Exodus 12:17-20 Syswerda, Jean, and Faith Organization.2001. NIV Women of Faith Study Bible: New International Version. Grand Rapids, Mich.: Zondervan.

Ref 7   Google search Question: What are the disadvantages of wood frames?

Ref 8   thesaurus.com

Ref 9   Exodus 13:16 Syswerda, Jean, and Faith Organization.2001. NIV Women of Faith Study Bible: New International Version. Grand Rapids, Mich.: Zondervan.

Ref 10   Exodus 13:17-18 Syswerda, Jean, and Faith Organization.2001. NIV Women of Faith Study Bible: New International Version. Grand Rapids, Mich.: Zondervan.

Ref 11   Keener, Craig S. 1993. *The IVP Bible Background Commentary New Testament.* Downers Grove. Ill. InterVarsity Press.

Ref 12   Hebrews 11:27 Syswerda, Jean, and Faith Organization.2001. NIV Women of Faith Study Bible: New International Version. Grand Rapids, Mich.: Zondervan.

Ref 13   Jakes, T.D, and Serita Ann Jakes. 2006. *T.D. And Serita Ann Jakes Speak to Women, 3-In-1.* Bethany house Publishers.

Ref 14   Exodus 14:3-7 Peterson, Eugene H. 1995. *The Message Bible.* Colorado Springs, Co: Navpress.

Ref 15   Maxwell, John C. 2007. *Talent Is Never Enough: Discover the Choices That Will Take You Beyond Your Talent.* Nashville, Tenn.: Thomas Nelson.

CHAPTER TWELVE

A Song of Salvation

'To take courage, you have to decide to go forward anyway.' [1]
BRUCE WILKINSON

Let's leave the Phoenix metaphor for a moment and talk turkey. The reason you exist is because something needs to be done that only you can do. It's as simple as that. And as straightforward as that seems, God chose you because He knows you have the determination to see it through. But what happens when your call to rise up isn't as smooth and uncomplicated as that? What if in your rising, you are met by doubters and sceptics, and critics, oh my! And just to throw a spanner in the works, what if those doubters and sceptics, and critics are the very same ones who did support your plan at the start, however, a steady beat of their minor key murmuring has caused them to go cold turkey on your ascending? What then? Well, God works all things out for good in our lives even when it looks bad, even when everything seems to be falling apart, even when something, or someone you feel needs fixing, even when you can't get over it, under it and there is no way around it, God *will* make a way. We need to understand that it is He, the One who made the stars and named each one of them, that fights our battles for us. And as we finally leave the dry road behind and head down the path toward the river we have to cross so we can continue onto the next phase of our warrior journey, you're possibly starting to grow quite fond of Miriam, our leader and prophetess, who is a living testament to God making a way when there was no way.

Perhaps you've been thinking about the water theme that runs through Miriam's life as your parched soul has thirsted for more of God as you walked along that dry road in the last chapter. However, now that we're heading down toward the river, it seems as we get closer and closer to its banks, Miriam is lost in her own thoughts. You watch her eyes as they scan the river for the best place to cross and you can hear she is humming a tune to herself. 'What's that song?' you ask as you feel its hypnotic melody lift your spirits out from under the wilderness way you've just experienced. Miriam stops humming for a moment and her cheeks flush slightly as she replies wistfully, 'It's a salvation song I sang long ago with my little brother.' You smile to yourself; you like the way Miriam speaks fondly of Moses. For we, who read the Exodus story, he is arguably the greatest biblical hero, but to Miriam, Moses will always be her baby brother. Strangely, the song she's confidently humming almost feels like a spontaneous worship moment, like a celebration of all God has done. Miriam puts words to the melody but the noise from the strong current of the river drowns out the song and you're only able to catch fragmented parts; '... The horse and its rider he has hurled into the sea... the Lord is my strength and my song... the Lord is a warrior...' From what bits you've heard of this song it certainly sounds like a great one to sing in church.

Turning the Tide

Ever since Miriam's teenaged years, the water motif had moved like a strong current throughout her life, setting into motion the courage Miriam needed so it helped her stop looking at her current circumstances and use the trials she was facing to push her up to a greater level of awareness of God's sovereignty, and in turn, turning the tide from her slavery mindset to obtaining the warrior within that brings with it the endurance to fight.[2] Pharaoh's plan to drown infants in the Nile had caused her to rise up at a young age as she sent her baby brother down the river in the basket their mother had prepared. We don't really know what happened to Jochebed, the mother of possibly the three greatest leaders in the Old Testament, Aaron, Miriam, and Moses. However, we know for a fact that she was a God-fearing woman who had a fearless faith that understood when warriors cannot see a way through, God provides, He rescues, He redeems, and He restores regardless of the lack of support from others. I sense Miriam carries her mother's tenacious spirit, and the song she's singing as we near the crossing of the river reminds you of everything God has brought you through. Whether it's battles in the fires of affliction or the enemy bringing a flood of adversaries, Miriam's leadership reveals we can come out from our trials better than before.[3]

When we trace our fingers over the lines that make up the scars from our past, they represent a boundary, an edge that limits the movements of our enemy. For those faded lines remind the devil to stay within the perimeters God has set around us as He promises to 'hem me in—behind and before because His hand is upon me.'[4] Faded scar tissue lets the devil know that warriors are able to rise up even from the dirtiest of ash piles he heaps upon us and we learn to spread our wings regardless of the fact we find ourselves knee deep in cinders, for our scars tell the testimonies of what God has brought us through.

Caught in the Current

Miriam still seems lost in her own thoughts now we're at the water's edge. Perhaps the memories from her past flood her mind as she leads us to the narrowest part of the river where you're hoping to see a boat of some description so we're able to cross safely to the other side of the river. You look along the riverbank, there is no boat, and the water current seems fairly strong and too deep for you to swim in. You hesitate for two reasons. Firstly, you'll admit that you're not that great a swimmer, and secondly, you were not planning on getting wet. Wondering how Miriam is going to navigate the crossing of the river, that familiar feeling of fear is slowly starting to rise up on the inside of you and you can sense it pulling you down by its strong current. It seems, in this moment, everything you've learned so far in your warrior journey has suddenly trickled out of you and you're trying desperately to mop up the mess. It's strange, but even in your fear and anxiety Psalm 46:10 keeps looping like an old familiar song in your head, *'Be still and know that I am God... Be still and know that I am God'*[5] repeating itself like a broken record. Easier said than done when your thoughts and emotions are churning around inside you like a washing machine on spin cycle. The suggestion of leaving you here at the riverbank because you feel like a complete failure, believing it's probably for the best if the journey is continued without you as you're clearly not cut out for this warrior gig, almost tumbles out of your mouth like a toddler who is learning how to walk, until Miriam notices your angst, sweaty palms, and shallow breathing. She leaves her water memories aside to comfort and reassure you as she sees the weight of worry on your disarmed shoulders has found you cursing to yourself over and over for giving into the fear that you thought you'd left behind in the little cabin in the forest. You look Miriam straight in the eye and say with every ounce of courage you can muster, 'If there is an easier way to become a warrior without crossing that river,' you sob, 'then sign me up. Otherwise, forget it!'

Hmmm...

The 'Didn't We Tell You' Society

If it's any help at all, Miriam knows exactly how you feel. Even after experiencing all the miracles in Egypt, even though the Israelites were free from the weight of Pharaoh's deity, the moment they reached the Red Sea's shoreline they suddenly panicked. 'As Pharaoh approached, the Israelites looked up and saw them—Egyptians! Coming at them! They were totally afraid. They cried out in terror to God. They told Moses, "Weren't the cemeteries large enough in Egypt so that you had to take us out here in the wilderness to die? What have you done to us, taking us out of Egypt? Back in Egypt didn't we tell you this would happen? Didn't we tell you, 'Leave us alone here in Egypt—we're better off as slaves in Egypt than as corpses in the wilderness.'"[6]

Well, Moses, you did try to free God's people, really you did.

Do you want to know what hinders the progress of a budding warrior more than any bleak circumstance they may be facing? It's listening to the wrong song. These melancholy voices can impede your flight path and stop your momentum as you are tempted to slow the pace to keep in step with the sound of their funeral march. Was Moses immune to the beat of the Israelites sombre song? I'll admit, this depressing chorus line could shake the confidence of even the greatest of Bible heroes. You see, the danger is if you listen to the wrong song then you start moving in the direction of its sound, leaving you wondering if God is going to make good on His promises. Sure, the Israelites had listened to Moses and followed God's plan to get them out of Egypt. They'd been inspired by Moses boldly initiating God's innovative ideas, even cheered him on and patted him on the back as Moses took his very first leap of faith and faced off Pharaoh. And yet, when their current circumstances looked nothing like what God had promised they believed there was no way around it—they were all doomed! In their mind they had become flightless birds, and their attitude was, 'Your great plan of rising up and escaping the daily grid was a pipe dream, Moses. We're not going to say we told you so, but didn't we tell you this would happen?'

Okay, let me just give you a word of advice before you look at that river and get sucked into a struggling-to-believe-you're-a-true-warrior-and-possibly-God-has-perhaps-made-a-huge-mistake-in-chosing-you-because-you-can't-see-a-way-through-this-problem-can't-see-a-way-around-it-and-you-feel-like-a-complete-failure, twisted kind of thinking. The bad news is you'll hear the wrong song many times on your warrior journey from the members of the 'Didn't We Tell You' society, who have matching club jackets with the motto, *'I Told You So'* embroidered in the fanciest font on the back. Accept they have club meets every time something blows up in your face, something didn't work out, or something didn't come through in the grand plan that God has for your life. And don't you dare laugh when these people tell you that they believe stepping out of your comfort zone is an extreme sport.

Still, the good news is that when people like that underestimate your ability to achieve something great for God, it is definitely to your advantage, dear warrior. As my own journey continues in leadership, I have concluded that warriors need to stop waiting for someone else's permission to do what God has called them to do, stop listening to songs of mourning from the naysayers, because God anoints His chosen ones for the task at hand. More on that in the next chapter. But for now, God is the only One whom we need to look toward for our worth, our value and our acceptance. God has called you out of the shadows to fulfill a specific purpose He has in mind and regardless of whether Pharaoh likes it or not, regardless of the club anthem from the 'Didn't We Tell You' society, you're going to keep flapping those wings toward your freedom and rise into all you need to be!

Power Move

We think we have to have it altogether for God to work though us, but we don't. God needed the Israelites to become a Nation, however, the first thing God needed to work on was their slave mentality so they could believe, with God's supernatural help, that they could become an army of warriors. God moved them to a place where they would see a miracle and know He was sovereign. All we need to know in our rising, dear warrior, is that if God has called us then nothing else matters. Jim Cymbala puts his two cents in this conversation as he proposes that 'God is attracted to weakness... our weakness makes room for His power.'[7] Yes! We need to view tight spots in our rising as places where our weakness is making room for God to show us His power.

The thing is, Pharaoh was plenty smart enough in his military training to notice that the Israelites were heading straight toward a rock and a hard place. He deemed their attempt to escape his rule as a joke because to him they looked like trapped animals with no place to go. Oh yes, his army would deter the Israelites from this uprising and have them all back in Egypt and under his taskmaster hand before drinks at sundown. Pharaoh viewed the Israelites as weak and incompetent, and he underestimated Yahweh's salvation power to set them free from under the Egyptian's rule. That's the great thing about God, He does His best work through our weaknesses as our inabilities give Him the space to move mightily. Listen, dear warrior, don't shelve your dreams just because of a few setbacks. God wants you to partner with Him as you keep moving forward from the slavery of your past and into the freedom of your future.

I want you to know that it's no good beating yourself up if you've discovered you've been listening to the wrong song, you're in good company. I tuned in for years to that death march frequency, however, if I'd have given into the fear and given up on my writing because I saw a river between myself and finding the right publisher then you wouldn't be reading this book right now. Again, in that prophecy spoken over me when I was fifteen, God told me I was a leader and, in that role, I had a responsibility. After many years of trials, I learned I needed to take that responsibility very seriously, and so I pressed in and trusted God to make a way when I saw no way because He was the One who had called me to be a leader. Amazingly, the most growth came in my weaknesses as they made me rely on God more.

Becoming a warrior doesn't happen overnight and it has taken me a lot of years to overcome self-doubt and all the struggles that come with the call of leadership. As Alli Worthington states, 'We are meant to grow, to become the people we are created to be, to continually be moving forward in our faith.'[8] I find it fascinating that the Israelites told Moses that they were 'better off as slaves in Egypt.' I'm sorry Israelites, I don't quite follow. You're saying that bondage, captivity, and enslavement is *better* than your freedom? And yet, we can adopt the same fear-based mindset when things get too hard, too difficult, or too scary. We believe it's better to have been left alone in our misery rather than pursue the unknown territory of what God has called us to do. We tend to blame the enemy for every blockage along our path, but the reality is that sometimes it's *we* who do all the self-sabotaging and forfeit our own freedom because, sure, we may be slaves for the rest of our lives, but it just *feels* more comfortable back in Egypt, right?!

The Invisible Becomes Visible

The great news is that Moses' confidence in who God said He was drowned out the Israelites chorus in questioning if God was going to make good on His promise to free them. 'And Moses said to the people, 'Do not be afraid. Stand still, and see the salvation of the Lord, which He will accomplish for you today. For the Egyptians whom you see today, you shall see again no more forever. The Lord will fight for you, and you shall hold your peace.'[9] As I shared at the start of our warrior journey, the enemy's attack is to crush and consume our confidence to gain the upper hand on us. And yet, when we choose to self-sabotage because we see no way forward in God's plan for our lives it is that cunning conquest the devil sees as a win. However, his *real* objective is for us to question God's character.

'And the Lord said to Moses, "Why do you cry to Me? Tell the children of Israel to go forward."' Some straight-shooting turkey talk from God right there, (which was possibly aimed at the 'Didn't We Tell You' society club members, by the way). 'But lift up your rod and stretch out your hand over the sea and divide it. And the children of Israel shall go on dry ground through the midst of the sea... then Moses stretched out his hand over the sea; and the Lord caused the sea to go back by a strong east wind all that night, and made the sea into dry land, and the waters divided.'[10] That power move should silence a few critics.

It's in this moment that Miriam starts humming the rhymical melody of her song once again as she has climbed up onto a ledge you hadn't noticed in your panic before. You decide to join her and see what she is excitedly pointing at. From the higher view the river's current is still moving fast, the water still looks cold and dark, but in spite of your nagging doubts you notice stepping stones just under the water that reach to the other side of the river. It's like everything you've been taught about igniting the warrior within comes flooding back into your mind and you remember what you learned along the wilderness way about what was once invisible becomes visible. Now you're looking at the problem from a higher perspective and it's caused everything to change. Take a deep breath and release it slowly, dear warrior, for you shall not be getting your feet wet today because God has made a way for you to keep moving forward. For this warrior journey is not about giving up, it's about giving in and surrendering to Him who not only named each one of the stars but counts them one by one.

Endnotes: Chapter Twelve

Ref 1   Wilkinson, Bruce. 2004. *The Dream Giver.* Global Vision Resources.

Ref 2   Farwell, Hanna. 2010. *The Sword and the Tamborine: Becoming a Warrior Through Worship.* Destiny Image Publishers.

Ref 3   Psalm 66:12 The Passion Translation: New Testament with Psalms, Proverbs, and Song of Songs, Second Edition. Passion & Fire Ministries, Inc. Broadstreet Publishing: 2018.

Ref 4   Psalm 139:5 Syswerda, Jean, and Faith Organization.2001. NIV Women of Faith Study Bible: New International Version. Grand Rapids, Mich.: Zondervan.

Ref 5   Psalm 46:10 Syswerda, Jean, and Faith Organization.2001. NIV Women of Faith Study Bible: New International Version. Grand Rapids, Mich.: Zondervan.

Ref 6   Exodus 14:10-12 Peterson, Eugene H. 1995. *The Message Bible.* Colorado Springs, Co: Navpress.

Ref 7   Cymbala, Jim, and (with Dean Merrill) *Fresh Wind, Fresh Fire: What happens when God's Spirit invades the hearts of his people.* 2003.

Ref 8   Worthington, Alli. 2018. *Fierce Faith: A woman's guide to fighting fear, wresting worry, and overcoming anxiety.*

Ref 9   Exodus 14:13-14 *Spiritual Warfare Bible.* 2012. Lake Mary, Florida, Charisma House.

Ref 10   Exodus 14:15-21 *Spiritual Warfare Bible.* 2012. Lake Mary, Florida, Charisma House.

CHAPTER THIRTEEN

Secondary Instrument

'If I thought I could win one more soul to the Lord by walking on my head and playing the tambourine with my toes, I'd learn how!' [1]
WILLIAM BOOTH

Now that you've crossed to the other side of the river, you feel different. You cannot explain what has changed but you know something has shifted. It seems that this part in our warrior journey feels the most symbolic so far as we've followed Miriam, moved out in faith, and placed our feet onto each stepping stone to cross the river. You sense the change has birthed something new within you and now you can't quite put your finger on the moment where your endless worry you experienced on the other side of the river has now been replaced with a deep need to worship. This rite of passage feels refreshing, like a baptism of fire that has tested your courage and set your feet on a foundation to trust in the One who made a way when you really thought there was none. At first, the exile felt like a gap, an estrangement in the journey to becoming a warrior and you struggled to join the dots. And despite your previous doubts in wondering if you'd ever have enough strength to rise up from the ashes of your past, you're starting to understand this exile, this parting, this segregation was God birthing something new within you. Now you feel the bondage of your past no longer defines who you are as you run your finger along the edge of your scars, and for some strange reason you just want to break out in song! Miriam gets excited at this growth in your journey and opens up the backpack. She pulls out a couple of tambourines as she wants to join in with your spontaneous worship moment.

Selah.

Believe me, your decreased enthusiasm as you stare aghast at the tambourines does not go unnoticed. I know, I totally get it, you sense your wave of shame is going to pull you under as quickly as the strong current of the river you've just crossed. So, for the sake of everyone's embarrassment, I can help you out a little here, as a cringeworthy 80's revival, tambourine waving worship moment was not what you had in mind. Am I right? But before you try and work out how you're going to silence those jingles, just go with me on this one.

Leading the Charge

Although Miriam is not mentioned along with her two brothers throughout the ten plagues in the Exodus out of Egypt, the pivotal role she played after the Israelites crossed the Red Sea is possibly the most well-known part of her story. Her celebrational tambourine waving isn't to make a song and dance out of what happened in church services during the 1980's. Oh no, this is the stuff of warrior legends.

'When Pharaoh's horses, chariots, and chariot-drivers drove into the sea, the Eternal caused the waters to collapse upon them. But the Israelites walked through the sea on dry ground. The prophetess, Miriam (Aaron's sister), picked up a tambourine, and all the rest of the women followed her with tambourines and joyful dancing. Sing to the Eternal One, for He has won a great victory; He has thrown the horse and its chariot into the sea.'[2]

The tambourine was a significant weapon against the enemy and was played for more reasons than just a joyful celebration. This percussion instrument was often used in warfare so an army would gain the courage to rise up as they went into battle.[3] When we read the Scriptures where the tambourine or timbrel is referenced, it was often the women who led the charge. In Judges we find Jephthah's daughter 'dancing to the sound of tambourines'[4] and in first Samuel we see the women celebrating David's return from killing Goliath 'with tambourines and lutes.'[5] Even the Psalms acknowledge the women as the tambourine players, 'Leaders in front, then musicians, with young maidens in between, striking their tambourines.'[6] Not only did Miriam lead the Israelites into a song of victory after witnessing Pharaoh and his army get engulfed by the chaotic waters of the Red Sea, but her bold action of warfare worship inspired other women to join in celebrating what God had done.

There is a knack to tambourine playing as 'when striking a tambourine, the player must know how and where to strike it in order to produce the desired effect.'[7] Oh, I believe Miriam knew where to strike to produce the desired effect of her tambourine playing alright. And as a woman, I have no doubt she possibly remembered the Israelites outfits in great detail as they left Egypt. I'll just refresh your memory, 'Be sure you are dressed and to go at a moment's notice—with sandals on your feet and a walking stick in your hand. Eat quickly because this is My Passover.'[8] Correct me if I'm wrong, but the Israelites were dressed ready for freedom which definitely gave those slaves a bit of elbowroom to move their chained mindsets from bondage to a freedom they'd never known as they chose to leave their enslaved past behind and step into the bright future God had planned for them. Are you dressed for freedom and ready to go at a moment's notice, dear warrior? Now you've crossed the river, do you feel covered enough in the freedom Jesus died for so you can leave your past in the past and step into the future God has for you? It's time, dear warrior, to take your tambourine, lead the charge for others to follow, and learn how and where to strike the enemy in order to produce the desired effect with your follow-up shot. I sense God has ignited something within you and as Lisa Bevere acknowledges, 'God has awakened His daughters to be so much more than soldiers. He is calling us to be warriors.'[9] Something for you to mull over while we attach ribbons to our timbrels.

The Silence is Deafening

While researching percussion instruments, I discovered why they are placed at the back of an orchestra. Percussion, by nature, is loud and can be overpowering for an audience and it is for this reason percussion instruments are placed at the back so it allows space to mellow the sound.[10] Interestingly, another reason why percussion is set up at the back of an orchestra is because percussionists are notorious for misbehaving.[10] As the warrior within is ignited, the enemy's new assignment is to make sure your sound ideas in rising are deterred from the volume being turned up on them. Although the enemy's aim is to silence you completely, he knows you've become too smart for that dirty little trick. No, what the devil will try to do is to mellow your sound by suggesting you stay at the back because you're far too loud and uncontrollable. He'll remind you that your misbehaving is becoming notorious and too distracting for others, so best if you hide, you know allow some space for things to settle as all this talk of rising is spiralling out of control. Sadly, his motives to silence women have gained a few supporters over the years and many warriors have been duped into submission without making a sound. However, there are a few women throughout history whose heroic actions the devil has not been able to silence, and we are still hearing the sound of their song long after they have departed this world. These women saw something needed to change and felt compelled to rise up regardless of the consequences.

I have to say that out of the long list of warrior women, Joan of Arc is still a favourite of mine. This fifteenth-century God fearing farm girl claimed to have heard voices from long departed saints and she eventually led the French army into many battles. And yet, in the course of time, she was put on trial at the tender age of nineteen because she was found to be guilty of the heresies she was falsely accused of and was burned at the stake. Her stirring words while the flames rose higher around her were a testament to her resolute faith in God and as her head dropped forward witnesses say that the name of Jesus was the final word that came from her lips.[11] Joan of Arc was a Phoenix for sure, whose bravery still rises from the flames to inspire others to take a stand for their faith.

Our enemy is very good at peddling his half-truths that drive a wedge between genders and his twisted revenge to silence women in the church is found in a Scripture that has caused many women warriors to fall on their sword. When reading Scripture, we need to understand the danger of taking a passage and analysing it by itself, as background, literary context, and the audience it was written for all need to be considered before we go jumping to any conclusions. Possibly the most infamous Scripture is found in the first letter to the Corinthians from the apostle Paul. He says in 1 Corinthians 14:33-34, 'As in all the congregations of the saints, women should remain silent in the churches. They are not allowed to speak, but must be in submission.'[12] Now, before you form a theology lynch mob and chase this apostle down because you believe he was against women ministering in the church, let me just clarify, that thought is far removed from what Paul was saying.

Let's look at this passage in more careful detail.

Paul's response was about bringing calm into the chaotic services that were occurring in the Corinthian Christian community, as God is not a God of chaos and disorder but of peace and order. Paul is not disallowing women to speak as the 'silent' he refers to is that the women are being disruptive.[13] We need to realise that men were used to listening to lectures as they were the only ones allowed to receive an education, so the women didn't know how to conduct themselves in a teaching setting and just talked right over the top of whoever was speaking.[13] Paul goes on to suggest a solution to the problem and offers that the women wait until they are in a private setting with their husband to ask their questions as the husband can help them with the instructions being taught. 'If they want to inquire about something, they should ask their own husbands at home; for it is disgraceful for a woman to speak in church.'[14] Paul's heart was for the Christian community to be respectful toward each other and be unified as 'everything should be done in a fitting and orderly way.'[15] Sadly, this passage of Scripture has been taught in error and silenced the voices of many women warriors who have felt called to the ministry. The enemy doesn't want others to rise up from the ashes, so women are told their call to preach and teach isn't biblical. Remember I mentioned earlier about listening to the wrong song? It's time some changed their tune and took some time to read the apostle Paul's other letters then they would notice he indorsed and encouraged women to be in ministry. I get sad when anointed, gifted women have so much to share and their sound is put on mute. Their silence has become deafening within the church body, and the enemy knows if the warrior is reignited within, they will become a threat to his scheming, as a chorus of warrior women who lead armies into battle with their tambourine song are a force to be reckoned with!

The Season for Hiding is Over

Just to clarify, God doesn't see women as secondary instruments to men and wrong biblical teaching must grieve God's heart for His daughters. Miriam's tambourine celebrational dance after crossing the Red Sea was her expression of worship to God, the One who made a way when there was none. I'm sure it was also a reminder to the enemy that he may have supressed, marginalised, and tried his hardest in stopping the Israelite women from rising up out of the slavery of their past, however, Miriam decided to make the move for she knew they were dressed for freedom and their destiny was not in the ashes. Staying silent and shrinking to the back of the orchestra because people have swallowed the devil's half-baked lies, telling women they are too loud and a misbehaved distraction, is a downright lie. Larry Sparks comments, 'When we restrict women from rising up and walking in the anointing to lead and prophesy, I believe we are—in part—restricting the Holy Spirit's movement on earth.'[16] God's secret follow-up shots are the women who walk in their God-given authority and do it faithfully alongside the men.

The season of your hiding is over, dear warrior, and now is the time to arise. God is calling you to rise up as He serenades you with His love song. Here, I'll let you listen to the melody of Song of Songs 2:10-13 for yourself.

'For now, is the time, my beautiful one.
The season has changed,
The bondage of your barren winter has ended,
And the season of hiding is over and gone.
The rains have soaked the earth
and left it bright with blossoming flowers.
The season for singing and pruning the vines has arrived.
I hear cooing of doves in our land,
Filling the air with songs to awaken you,
And guide you forth.
Can you not discern this new day of destiny
breaking forth around you?
The early signs of my purposes and plans are bursting forth.
The budding vines of new life are now blooming everywhere.

> The fragrance of their flowers whispers,
> "There is a change in the air."
> Arise, my love, my beautiful companion,
> And run with me to the higher place.
> For now, is the time to arise and come away with me.'[17]

The season has changed and the time for hiding is over and gone, precious firebird. Don't listen to the sound of the enemy's lies and stay hidden in the ashes, for others are counting on you to rise up and lead the charge as they head toward the battles. Listen in, dear warrior, and pay attention to His calling, for a change is in the air.

Prayer

Dear God,

I don't want my past to define my future. Comfort me where I've felt neglected, disappointed and let-down by relationships. Even in my stumbling, dazed confusion as things seemed to keep blowing up in my face, You never turned Your back on me, You never left me or abandoned me, and if I thought You did leave me alone, forgive me for believing that lie.

It is right here in the exile, the gap, the transition where I discovered that I am not a secondary instrument but a God-chosen instrument and it was in this difficult transition where You, Lord, have started to transform me into the warrior I needed to become. Thank you that You led me through the waters so I was able to allow You the space to rebirth and reignite something inside of me that has possibly lay dormant for years.

Forgive me in the moments I didn't trust You to make a way when I thought there was none. Thank you for Your grace that gave me enough courage for me to test out my wings and confidently rise up from the ashes. My flight path from slavery to freedom is guided by Your everlasting light and careful hand. Tracing my fingers over the lines that make up the scars of my past remind me of the times I listened to the wrong song instead of Your voice, Your call. You are always encouraging me to keep rising and You do it so that others are able to follow the sound of Your heartbeat. As it is here in the exile where I have learned warrior's need to stop listening to the death march and dance to a different beat.

Amen.

Endnotes: Chapter Thirteen

Ref 1   Website: quotes.com

Ref 2   Exodus 15:19-21. Ecclesia Bible Society. 2012. *The Voice Bible: Step into the Story of Scripture.* Nashville: Thomas Nelson

Ref 3   timbrelpraise.org/background/tambourine-in-the-bible/

Ref 4   Judges 11:34. Syswerda, Jean, and Faith Organization.2001. NIV Women of Faith Study Bible: New International Version. Grand Rapids, Mich.: Zondervan.

Ref 5   1 Samuel 18:6. Syswerda, Jean, and Faith Organization.2001. NIV Women of Faith Study Bible: New International Version. Grand Rapids, Mich.: Zondervan.

Ref 6   Psalm 68:25 The Passion Translation: New Testament with Psalms, Proverbs, and Song of Songs, Second Edition. Passion & Fire Ministries, Inc. Broadstreet Publishing: 2018.

Ref 7   Tambourine: What is a tambourine? (Definition and history of tambourine musical instrument) June 24, 2018, by CMUSE.   Webpage: cmuse.org/tambourine/

Ref 8   Exodus 12:11. Ecclesia Bible Society. 2012. *The Voice Bible: Step into the Story of Scripture.* Nashville: Thomas Nelson

Ref 9   Bevere, Lisa. 2013. *Girls With Swords: How to carry your cross like a hero.* Colorado Springs, Colorado: Waterbrook Press.

Ref 10   soundsfunny.org/why-percussion-instruments-at-the-back-of-orchestra/

Ref 11   Sackville-West, V. 1955. *Saint Joan of Arc: A rational and open-minded study giving clearly and simply the main historical facts about the life of this fifteenth-century shepherd girl who saved her country.* Penguin books.

Ref 12   1 Corinthians 14:33-34. Syswerda, Jean, and Faith Organization.2001. NIV Women of Faith Study Bible: New International Version. Grand Rapids, Mich.: Zondervan.

Ref 13   White, Adam. 2023. 1st and 2nd Corinthians Subject. Alphacrucis University College.

Ref 14   1 Corinthians 14:35. Syswerda, Jean, and Faith Organization.2001. NIV Women of Faith Study Bible: New International Version. Grand Rapids, Mich.: Zondervan.

Ref 15   1 Corinthians 14:38. Syswerda, Jean, and Faith Organization.2001. NIV Women of Faith Study Bible: New International Version. Grand Rapids, Mich.: Zondervan.

Ref 16   Sparks, Larry, and Patricia King. 2018. *Arise: A prophetic call for women to receive swords, mantles, and kingdom assignments.* Destiny Image Publishers.

Ref 17   Song of Songs 2:10-13. The Passion Translation: New Testament with Psalms, Proverbs, and Song of Songs, Second Edition. Passion & Fire Ministries, Inc. Broadstreet Publishing: 2018.

PART THREE

THE SONG

CHAPTER FOURTEEN

Lead By Example

'A song is rising within me.
A song of Your faithfulness and love.'[1]
BRIAN SIMMONS & GRETCHEN RODRIGUEZ

The older I get, the more I have come to realise that I am a verbal processor. It's how I figure stuff out, look at ideas from a different perspective and try to make sense of the world around me. However, whether muttering to myself or sharing my concerns with others, my verbal processing can sometimes quickly descend into a lament as I yammer and whine, sounding off like a screeching siren for everyone to hear. When I get like that, I feel like such a complainer, so I haul myself out of that dark hole and go in the total opposite direction, keeping quiet, not speaking out, internalising my thoughts so they swirl around inside of me like a foreboding storm, until my lament has percolated into the very fibre of my being. Either way isn't healthy. Balance is needed.

We tend to focus on the fresh wings of the Phoenix as a necessity for its flight out of the ashes, and indeed without its wings the Phoenix could never learn how to fly. Be that as it may, it is the tail that helps the firebird to brake, gain balance and change directions.[2]

Whenever I feel overwhelmed and out of sorts and the cold winds in the barren wilderness cause me to catch my breath, making me a little wobbly in my rising, my friend always gives me some uplifting words to help settle my franticly flapping wings to a gentler glide. 'Well,' she wisely offers, 'it's okay to complain and grumble to help with your thought processing, as long as the conversation ends on a positive note. As long as you can find one good thing to say about who you're complaining about, you'll find that it's not so bad after all.' Oh, that's good. If we're to stay out of the ashes and rise up, we really need to start singing a different tune and not allow our negative thoughts to nosedive into a tailspin. Another wise person once said that transformation is a process and not an event. Oh, that's good too. Some sound advice, right there. The thing is, God called Miriam to leadership from a young age and in the process of her growing up, the calling ignited the prophetess within her as God gave Miriam more and more responsibility so she could rise slowly into the warrior God had intended her to become.

Shake Your Tail Feathers

When we glean from the leadership lessons of Aaron, Miriam, and Moses we wonder if it was the events of the miracles that shaped them as leaders, and in some way I believe the miracles played a part in their rising. And yet, I can't help but notice when

I read the process of the Exodus to exile in Scripture, these leaders led the Israelites out of Egypt and lived with God's chosen people for many years right through the barrenness of the desert plains, and it was this process where the tail feathers of their plumage were grown and developed so these three firebird leaders could rise to the next level of their leadership.

Starting at the tail end of their song of rising taught them how to brake, gain balance and change direction in their thinking, as it was in the unseen moments where they learned how to shake their tail feathers and become mighty warriors for God. It says in Proverbs 20:5 that 'knowing what is right is like deep water in the heart; a wise person draws from the well within'[3] and as Miriam's life theme is water, we're going to go with that thought. For I am sure witnessing the many miracles God performed to help the Israelites escape the Egyptians tyranny that stemmed from Pharaoh's rule, Miriam had learned to draw deeply from her relationship with God, so she was able to lead well. However, her pivotal moments were when God promoted Miriam in the unnoticed and concealed stages of her rising that raised her to another level of leadership.

As I mentioned in my previous book, *Wounded and on the Run*, I attended a women's leadership conference a few years ago that was specifically tailored for women preachers, and it totally ignited a fire within my soul. I remember in one of the sessions, Pastor Vicki Simpson talked about paying the price in the call of leadership and said that some things cannot be imparted by laying on of hands or prayer, some things are entrusted to us progressively, and although the gifts of God are free, there is a price we need to pay and each price is unique to our calling. She went on to say that we don't always make the connection between our anointing and the pain found in being obedient to what God has called us to do, as every major promotion is usually preceded by a tough season.[4] And boy, that is so true, as in my own leadership journey I have found with each breakthrough and advancement of my rising, it has always followed with a tough season. However, these were the seasons where God taught me to practice using my tail feathers to brake, gain balance, and change direction, so I could continue to rise into all He had waiting for me. The enemy finds it disturbing when his assaults and arrows are reversed because we've discovered our tail is the rudder that steers us up from the ashes and into our freedom. Warriors take note, if we want our follow-up shot to be effective on the enemy then we need to make sure that our song starts at the tail end so we can finish on a high note.

A Song of Lament

We need to understand that peaceful times do not make warriors. For it's in the fray, the ruckus of the rumble, and the skirmishes of tiff and tussle where we learn our most valuable lessons. God is always calling His warriors to grow and mature, and we do most of our strength training through the daring challenges He presents to us as we move through the furnace of affliction. Because God knows that the more you grow, the more His power is able to flow through you, and in turn, satisfises your heart and transforms your world and others around you. Let me just be clear, this ain't no, *fake it till you make it* chapter as I teach you how to pack up all your feelings in a box and hide them in a dimly lit basement somewhere, pretending everything and everyone is totally awesome. That kind of bogus Christianity is nauseating, and it doesn't bring any depth to your faith.

Covering, muffling, and withholding truth's sound when we feel the need to speak up and speak out from a deep love for God's people, voicing something that just doesn't feel right, is where we can be duped into believing that we're the problem, so our voice eventually gets silenced. Trust me, betrayal, lies, and cover ups only lead to more grief and heartache than if we'd have just been completely honest and opened up about what was bothering us in the first place. Sure, ripping off a Band-Aid isn't pleasant, but to heal our wounds we need to let some fresh air circulate so the healing can start, and the wounds don't have a chance in hell to fester.

A song of lament is not a melody we warriors are willingly ready to put up our hand and sing to, as we much prefer to learn the song of rising for when we emerge from the flames, pumping our fist in the air like Rocky Balboa, triumphant in our victory. I get it, you're becoming a little impatient in your rising, but slow down there, speed racer firebird, as wisdom needs to come with your calling. Trust me, it will be worth the wait. But for now, your song needs some downbeats for pace, it needs some richness in its rhythm so the tempo is just right. I know what you're thinking, we are starting our follow-up shot song on a low note. Trust Miriam's leading, as starting here, in the lament, means we can rise together in God's strength as your words need to match God's rhythm. So, are you ready for the next phase of our journey? Good. Glad we're singing from the same song sheet.

Tempo and Rhythm

God is not a God of chaos but of order, and an organised follow-up shot will be far more effective on our enemy than a song that has no beats. I do hope you'll gain some pace as you learn how to use your tail feathers in this song of lament as I want you to rise well, dear warrior, and over the next few chapters, we shall be looking at each of the seven elements of music. [5] The first two are tempo and rhythm and it is these two elements that often work together in a song creating the 'backbone' as it helps the listener to perceive and engage with a piece of music.[6] When listening to a ballad, it draws out different emotions compared to an up tempo dance track, as the rhythm and tempo in a song are there to evoke different responses.[6] I know all you optimistic, positive sanguine personality types are desperately wanting to get to the praise break, high-energy banger, but if we want to lead by example then we'll need to develop some backbone in our song, taking the beats down a notch and start with a ballad, a lament, so we can build up the momentum further down the track. In Isaiah 45:2-3, the prophet gives us the full richness of restoration that is found in God, 'I will go before you and will level the mountains; I will break down gates of bronze and cut through bars of iron. I will give you the treasures of darkness, riches stored in secret places, so that you may know that I am the Lord, the God of Israel, who summons you by name.'[7] Oh, what treasures, Lord are You wanting to give Your warriors in the darkest moments of our journey? Where can we find these riches that are stored in secret places, so we may know that You are Lord?

Our response to the slow rhythmic tempo of a good lament is important for our song as Peter Scazzero notes, 'we mistakenly believe embracing our grief will slow us down and hinder us in achieving God's mission in the world. Actually, the opposite is true. Embracing our losses, God's way, actually advances his mission.'[8] I don't know about you, but I have struggled over the years through my fear of abandonment to let God take full control of every beat of my life. I have learned over the years that trying to control the rhythm and tempo parts of our song are not up to us, as it is God who sets the pace in our rising. When we read most of the rhythmical, songlike Psalms of David's we find he starts his songs in the tempo of lament and rises up to the rhythm of praise and worship. We realise when reading them that he learned far more in the ashes of his cave dwelling years than anywhere else in his story as he had to totally rely on God for his protection and provision which developed his poetry into praise, prayer, wisdom, prophecy, and the poetry of Christ.[9] These songlike Psalms give us a glimpse into the rhythm and tempo that helped fuel and ignite David into a warrior. And as he learned to allow the grief and loss he felt over his relationship with Saul to grow his tail feathers for him to rise, he was able to brake, gain balance and change direction in his lament, steering his flight path from weeping into praising. Read David's poetic Psalm 30 as the rhythm and tempo of his song ebbs and flows.

'Lord, I will exalt you and lift you high,
For you have lifted me up on high!
Over all my boasting, gloating enemies,
You made me triumph.
O Lord, my healing God,
I cried out for a miracle and you healed me!
You brought me back from the brink of death,
From the depths below.
Now here I am, alive and well, fully restored!
O sing and make melody, you steadfast lovers of God.
Give thanks to him every time you reflect on his holiness!
I've learned that his anger lasts for a moment,

> But his loving favour lasts a lifetime!
> We may weep through the night,
> But at daybreak, it will turn into shouts of ecstatic joy.
> I remember boasting, 'I've got it made!
> Nothing can stop me now!
> I'm God's favoured one; he's made me steady as a mountain!'
> But then suddenly, you hid your face from me.
> I was panic-stricken and became depressed.
> Still, I cried out to you, Lord God.
> I shouted out for mercy, saying,
> 'What would you gain in my death,
> If I were to go down in the depths of darkness?
> Will a grave sing your song?
> How could death's dust declare your faithfulness?'
> So, hear me now, Lord; show me your famous mercy.
> O God, be my saviour and rescue me!
> Then he broke through and transformed all my wailing
> Into a whirling dance of ecstatic praise!
> He has torn the veil and lifted from me,
> The sad heaviness of mourning.
> He wrapped me in the glory garments of gladness.
> How could I be silent when it's time to praise you?
> Now my heart sings out loud, bursting with joy—
> A bliss inside that keeps me singing,
> I can never thank you enough!' [10]

Remember, God entrusts us with responsibility progressively as every major promotion is usually preceded by a tough season and when we learn to trust God with the rhythm and tempo of our song we can rise well. This is the training ground for warriors as we practise using our tail feathers to gain balance and change direction in our lament, as we learn to speak out and do it God's way and in His timing. This helps our wounds to stay healed and closed. I totally understand the memory of emotions when you look at your scars for they tell parts of your story you'd rather forget, but this is where the flow and movement of our follow-up shot gains acceleration against the enemy. Joseph reminds us in Genesis 50:19-20 that it is not our place to judge others even though what they did to us was to harm us, 'Am I to judge instead of God? It is not my place. Even though you intended to harm me, God intended it only for good, and through me, He preserved the lives of countless people, as He is still doing today.'[11]

I am a living testament to God's restoring process as He used my deepest wounds to build a little cabin deep in the forest so others could find their healing and restoration. Believe me, no amount of rejection, humiliation, regret, or mistakes can separate us from God's loving embrace, and we can easily forget the strength we found in the process of Jesus listening to our lament while He lovingly cleaned wounds and soothed fears in that little cabin in the woods. As Ann Voskamp acknowledges, 'If our lips never speak those fears out loud—the fears remain slippery... turning our hearts away from Love Himself.'[12] Oh Lord, please don't let our hearts turn away from You as we try to control, cover up, and quieten the lamenting rhythms of our song so it sounds pitch perfect to others around us. The trouble with wounded warriors is we've believed the lie that suppressing our feelings is a foolproof way for the follow-up shot to work effectively. We're convinced it's the perfection of the shot that scares our enemy into submission because he can find no holes or cracks within our faith. However, it is in the broken pieces of our lamenting prayers where our follow-up shot gains enough speed to pinpoint the hiding places with honest accuracy, so the enemy's dark schemes are exposed to God's light.

Behaving Like Orphans

Another word for lament is sing[13] and Miriam wants you to see that your song of rising brings with it a new way of thinking as your lament is where you can fully depend on God to help you rise up through the flames of affliction. She understands that the reason God gives you things progressively is because too much too soon will cause you to drop the ball and you'll find you're back in the ashes of despair, falsely believing you're a failure.

At this point we pick up the Israelites story again in Exodus chapter 16, as God's people are now a few short weeks into their journey toward the Promised Land. Even though God showed His power and sovereignty through each of the ten plagues and miraculously parted the Red Sea so Pharaoh and his army along with his horses and chariots were drowned, it didn't take long for the Israelites to lament because they had to move from the oasis of Elim, 'where there was 12 fresh water springs and 70 palm trees with dates and enter into the desert of sin, which was located between Elim and Sinai.'[14] This part of their journey was going to take much longer than anyone expected. See, that's the thing with situations that cause us to complain and lament, they take much longer than we expect but this is where you learn to trust God to bring you through the rhythm and tempo of your song, dear warrior, as your follow-up shot is going to resound and vibrate straight into the enemy's camp. So, why was everyone complaining? Well, we can wave a knowing finger at the Israelites for all their constant complaining. I mean, the nerve of them! After all God had done for them to bring them out of Egypt.

We would *never* act like that.

Would we?

Bill Johnson picked up on this kind of thinking when he said, 'Orphans live differently from children who know they're loved.'[15] Oh my, that kind of quote can knock the rhythm and tempo right out of your song, as I have lost count the number of times I have acted like an orphan rather than a child of God because I didn't feel loved. To be perfectly honest with you, I can still allow my lamenting prayers to question God, and I've done it so many times as I keep asking Him if He is going to pull through on the provision, needing His help so I am able to rise into what He has called me to do. Tut, tut, tut, Wendy, still struggling with abandonment issues, and *you're* the one who wrote a book on overcoming your wounding? *Please*.

See that's the sticking point. The enemy is so hellbent on making sure you stay in those ashes permanently, dear firebird, that he'll keep on reminding you there is no point in putting in all that effort into rising because your past wounding will always keep you falling for his lies, so the knock-on effect is you'll keep failing to see how much God loves you. 'Admit it', he'll whisper, when you're feeling at your lowest point, 'you're a flightless bird whose dreams of one day becoming a Phoenix, believing their glorious rising will go down in a blaze of glory, is in actual fact going to go down in a fireball of flames, not glory, as you keep getting stuck into orphan mentality.' When we have the tenacity and bravery to rise, the enemy always tries to set us up for a great fall. And regardless of how well you can flap your wings and use those tail feathers to rise from the ashes, dear Phoenix, your rising will get the enemy all in a tizzy if you suddenly realise that you're *not* an orphan after all. For he knows when you become a true warrior, who understands in the core of their being how much God loves them, there'll be no stopping you when you realise your follow-up shot is coming *from* the victory that Jesus already won at the cross.

Flying Light

The Israelites seemed to be running on empty and they complained to their leaders. 'As soon as they got to the desert of Sin, the entire community of Israelites complained to Moses and Aaron. 'It would have been better if we had died by the hand of the Eternal in Egypt. At least we had plenty to eat and drink, for our pots were stuffed with meat and we had as much bread as we wanted. But now you have brought the entire community out to the desert to starve us to death.' Oh, my goodness, they are *still* going on about how 'good' they had it in Egypt! This is how an orphan mindset messes with your mind. Israelites listen to what you are saying. You believe you were better off in Egypt? May I remind you that you were SLAVES in Egypt! Alright, okay, let's not get in a flap over their complaining. To be fair, I'll accept the Israelites were perhaps a little 'hangry' as I do tend to get irritable myself when I haven't eaten for a while. Apparently, being hangry is a real thing according to experts, as the mixture of hunger and anger blended releases a hormone adrenaline to raise your glucose to a normal level.[17] I love how the next line in the Exodus story says, 'God speaks to Moses.' Yes, a warrior is needed to calm all those complainers down. 'Look! I will cause bread to rain down from heaven for you, and the people will go out and gather a helping of it each day. I will test them to see if they are willing to live by My instructions... rest assured, I have heard the constant complaining of the Israelites.'[18] Oh, my lord, rest assured we have too!

However, let me ask you a question. Are you flying light? What I mean, is your faith hungry enough to see God move miraculously in your life? The whole theme of the Exodus to exile adventure was that God provided for His people as He heard their complaints and sent provision. 'That evening, quail flew in and covered the camp; and when morning arrived, what seemed to be ordinary dew was all around the camp. But when the dew evaporated, it left behind a thin, mysterious, flaky substance that looked like frost on top of the dry desert ground. The people of Israel went out to examine it. They had never seen anything quite like it. 'What is it?'[18] The people didn't have a clue what this strange substance was. 'It is bread which the Eternal has given you to eat.' The English translation for the word, 'manna' is 'what is it?'[19] We need to recognise that it is fear that fuels our complaining, as we wonder if God is going to provide His manna to feed our hungry souls. Over the years, I have experienced all manner of heartbreaks and each time I thought my faith would starve to death. But time and time again, even in my complaining, orphan mindset, God is so faithful to His children, and He sent His manna and provided me with whatever provision I needed to keep me rising up into what He had asked me to do. Betrayal, debt, and slander are just a few heartaches where I have felt a deep sense of abandonment, causing me to stay in the ashes for the longest time instead of rising. I remember when God asked me to take another scary step in my calling. What do you think I did? Well, I went straight into my prayer closet, closed the door, and... complained. Do you know what God shot back with? 'Wendy, why can't you just do something I've asked you to do without complaining about it?'

Ouch!

It's so easy for warriors to romanticise about their calling. We get a word from God, asking us to rise up and then we falsely believe that we aren't going to experience any barren, wilderness moments along our journey. We just want to snap our fingers and find ourselves in the Promised Land enjoying all that milk and honey. However, God needs to make sure we are willing to live by His instructions first. We have got to be hungry enough to believe for His provision before we can rise into all He has for us. God wants us to completely rely on Him to set the rhythm and tempo, for a song is rising within us and it's a song of God's faithfulness and love.

Endnotes: Chapter Fourteen

Ref 1   Simmons, Brian, and Gretchen Rodriguez. 2023. Encounter God's heart... A Song Is Rising in the Wilderness. "The Vision"

Ref 2   Google.com Question Search 'What helps birds balance and fly?'

Ref 3   Proverbs 20:5. Peterson, Eugene H. 1995. *The Message Bible.* Colorado Springs, Co: Navpress.

Ref 4   Simpson, Vicki. 2015. 'She's The Voice' Women's Conference. C3 Church/Own notes

Ref 5   phoenixsymphony.org Google search question 'What are the elements of a song?'

Ref 6   Miraglia, Dusti. 'Rhythm Vs Tempo: Exploring The Foundations Of Emotion And Energy In Music.' May 15th, 2021. Website: unison.audio

Ref 7   Isaiah 45:2-3. Syswerda, Jean, and Faith Organization.2001. NIV Women of Faith Study Bible: New International Version. Grand Rapids, Mich.: Zondervan.

Ref 8   Scazzero, Peter. 2021. *Emotionally Healthy Discipleship: Moving from shallow Christianity to Deep Transformation.* Grand Rapids, Mich.: Zondervan.

Ref 9   Psalms Commentary introduction, author and audience and major themes. The Passion Translation: New Testament with Psalms, Proverbs, and Song of Songs, Second Edition. Passion & Fire Ministries, Inc. Broadstreet Publishing: 2018.

Ref 10   Psalm 30. The Passion Translation: New Testament with Psalms, Proverbs, and Song of Songs, Second Edition. Passion & Fire Ministries, Inc. Broadstreet Publishing: 2018.

Ref 11   Genesis 50:19-20. Ecclesia Bible Society. 2012. *The Voice Bible: Step into the Story of Scripture.* Nashville: Thomas Nelson

Ref 12   Voskamp, Ann. 2022. *Waymaker : Finding the Way to the Life You've Always Dreamed Of.* Nashville, Tennessee: W Publishing Group, An Imprint Of Thomas Nelson.

Ref 13   thesaurus.com

Ref 14   Exodus 15:27, Exodus 16:1. Ecclesia Bible Society. 2012. *The Voice Bible: Step into the Story of Scripture.* Nashville: Thomas Nelson.

Ref 15   Johnson, Bill. 2018. *God is Good: He's better than you think.* Destiny Image Publishers.

Ref 16   Exodus 16:2-3. Ecclesia Bible Society. 2012. *The Voice Bible: Step into the Story of Scripture.* Nashville: Thomas Nelson.

Ref 17   health.com 'What happens when you get hangry?'

Ref 18   Exodus 16:4 -12. Ecclesia Bible Society. 2012. *The Voice Bible: Step into the Story of Scripture.* Nashville: Thomas Nelson.

Ref 19   Google Search question. What does manna mean?

CHAPTER FIFTEEN

Big Sister

'If your sister is in a tearing hurry to go out and cannot catch your eye, she's wearing your best sweater.'[1]
PAM BROWN

A bird sings in one of the trees in our garden some mornings. I'm not sure whether it's a native bird to Australia or one that was introduced, but its song sounds just like the birds I used to hear back in England. This birdsong evokes childhood memories of my sister and I going on bike rides with our mum. On the mornings we decided the weather would hold out for a bike ride, mum would always make a packed lunch for our adventure as she couldn't afford café prices, and we set off taking full advantage of the long, warm, summer days, biking to different villages with our sun-kissed faces enjoying the cool breeze while we whizzed down hills with our legs out stretched from the bike pedals, laughing, and having fun. Believe it or not, church graveyards were mainly our go-to spot for lunch where mum would find a large patch of grass or a bench to set up our picnic. Starving from our bike ride, my sister and I eagerly waited until mum handed out all her infamous homemade cheese and cucumber crusty rolls, (she told us that she brought rolls because sandwich bread always went soggy, plus she used cucumber instead of tomatoes as they always made the bread soggy too), followed by a bag of crisps each and a large bottle of pop (soda, if you prefer) which was carefully measured out into three small plastic cups.

Cemeteries always fascinated my sister and I, and after our picnic lunch we would often end up walking around the graveyard reading the date of each headstone to see who could find the oldest one first. Although it may seem a little odd to have a picnic in a church graveyard, we chose this setting because it was quiet, peaceful. A place to think, and a space to reset. Also, my sister and I loved the fact that our mum always encouraged our made-up stories about the people we read about on the headstones which only fuelled our imaginations further. I remember in one church graveyard, all the headstones were facing the village and only one of them was facing the other way. This caused our imaginations to run wild as we concocted an amazing story as to why this person was deemed unworthy to face the village, even in death. I remember in high school a rumour going around that the headstone marked with the skull and cross bones that was in our local parish graveyard, would seep blood through the large crack in the stone on Halloween night because it was rumoured to be the grave of a pirate. Of course, none of this was true. However, stories tend to gain traction when you pitch it to someone well, and before you know it you end up with a fable that is chock full of untruths which gets passed down from one generation to the next.

Pitch. This is the third element of the seven that make up a good song and it is an essential component, playing a crucial role in the emotional impact and the overall quality of a performance. The higher the pitch the more elation and excitement, lower pitch produces sadness.² Stories are a powerful tool to pass down truths to the next generation, and this is perhaps why God made sure that the Israelites told the story that it was He who rescued them from the land of Egypt over and over again, so that the generations to come would remember what God had done for them. So, seeing as we're talking about picnics and resting places, perhaps this is a good time to take another break, open up the backpack and pass round the cheese and cucumber rolls, as Miriam shares the story of how her younger brother, Aaron, became the first high priest.

Consecration

Goodness, are we *finally* going to talk about Miriam's other brother, Aaron? Yes, we're already halfway into our journey and he's been patiently waiting for his big sister to share his part in the Exodus story since we left the little cabin in the forest, as we headed out on our warrior adventure. Warriors have a lot to learn from Aaron, and as Miriam has led us slowly and carefully into the Exodus and onto the exile, now she is taking us through the elements that make up our follow-up shot song. Here is where we learn some lessons from Aaron's style of leadership, as this part of the story is where Aaron gets to be centre stage. To set the scene, Moses has shared with the Israelites the Ten Commandments and all the other instructions and specifications from God on how His people should live and how they should build the tabernacle. 'Moses then went and told the people exactly what the Eternal had said, as he carefully laid out and repeated God's instructions. 'All the people answered as if they had one, single voice. "We will do all that the Eternal has asked us to do!"' [3] Moses must have pitched God's instructions to the Israelites well, as amazingly, this time there are no complaints. They each pitched in, bringing their gifts and skill sets to build the tabernacle, a holy sanctuary in God's honour for rescuing them out of Egypt, a place where He could dwell among His people.[4] Now that the tabernacle was complete, Moses gives instructions about making the people holy and ordaining a priesthood, to the service of God.[5] The priesthood was a mark that the religious system was starting to mature and God singled out Aaron and his sons to serve in the priesthood, establishing an office that was to become the succession for the generations of high priests to come.[5] Special garments were worn by the priests as they were held to a higher standard of obedience by God. Failure to perform their duties or provide a proper example led to a swift punishment by God as the priest's responsibility was to be the people's representative.[5] 'Have your brother, Aaron, and his sons (Nadad, Abihu, Eleazar, and Ithamar) brought to you and appoint them to serve Me as priests for the people of Israel. In order to reflect the glory and beauty of their office, create sacred garments for your brother, Aaron. Talk with all the skilled workers—those whom I have gifted with talent and the spirit of wisdom—and instruct them to create distinct garments that set Aaron apart from the others whenever he is serving Me as priest.'[6]

Aaron's ceremonial garments were covered with the names of the tribes of Israel as a reminder of their holy calling, and also, a reminder to God. It's not that God would ever forget, but there are times and seasons when heaven's song seems silent while God's people suffer and God remembers His promises that He rescues His people, so, the detailed robes of the high priest's apparel resound and echo key aspects of God's relationship with His people.[7] God took His own sweet time in carefully laying out every detail and instruction to Moses. He doesn't rush through them, as no less than four chapters are dedicated to each specific part of the priestly service. Other words for consecration are anointing, blessing, making holy[8] and when warriors realise they are 'a chosen people, set aside to be a royal order of priests, a holy nation, God's own; so that you may proclaim the wonderous acts of the One who called you out of inky darkness into shimmering light' [9] we can boldly proclaim the wonderous acts of the One who called us and confidently move into His shimmering light. This certainly feels like the pitch to our song is rising well, don't you think? For the story we tell in our own lives needs to not only be filled with God's truth but also be orderly. This way we'll be able to judge the sound of God's ordered voice through the enemy's chaotic lies.

It is vital warriors listen to the heartbeat of God so the pitch in each of the higher and lower sounds help us to rise up from the ashes, leaving our past behind and aim our song straight at enemy territory. When we can feel the beat of God's heart, we hear what He hears, we feel what He feels, and we see what He sees. In my prayer times, I frequently ask God to break my heart for breaks His so I can tune into His heartbeat, so my song raises the battle cry toward the enemy. As Jill Austin states 'If you know the heart of God, then you can also awaken your heart for the people around you... because you catch the dream, the dream of God.'[10] Right on, sister! Because our calling isn't just for our own awakening but for other firebirds who are struggling to rise up from chaos of the ashes. As Aaron and his sons served in the priesthood, it established a song, a story, a truth for the next generation to rise into.

White Noise

High and low frequencies make up a pitch, however, white noise contains all frequencies and can mask other sounds.[11] Now, that's interesting, and I do hope this little piece of information has pricked your ears up, as it sure sounds like one of the enemy's tactics. He'll do his best to get us busy listening to all the frequencies that make up the white noise in an attempt to mask or drown out the frequency of God's voice, so he can laugh at our downfall as we tail spin into the ashes of anxiety and worry until we're an unholy hot mess. Sadly, if we listen long enough to the enemy's noisy distractions our song will become restricted and eventually prevent us from rising. The devil knows when we start to feel life's pressures we turn down and eventually tune out of God's specific instructions that are designed to help us rise, and his schemes make sure there will be no Phoenix rising up out of the flames, just the remains of yet another burnt-out warrior on the battlefield. Our rising can get side tracked all too easily and we can forget the story of how God rescued us from the ashes of Egypt unless the story keeps getting retold. Listen in, dear warrior, we cannot rise unless we resist the devil. How do you purpose we do that? Well, James reminds us that we need to *submit* to the One true God and fight against the devil and his schemes.[12] Another version of that same Scripture says, 'and he will flee from you.'[13] Sounds like the pitch to a song which can evoke memories to a story that reveals God's truth. Hang in there, firebird, your song is going dispel the darkness and illuminate your world!

Your Wardrobe is My Wardrobe

My songbird at the start of this chapter that evoked childhood memories of bike rides and eating lunches in church graveyards sounds like my big sister and I never argued or fought. Well, I'd love to say that we never did, and for the most part, we got on reasonably well growing up. However, my sister is four years older than me and naturally she finished school before I did, which meant that she started work before I did, which meant she had money to buy new clothes—like, on the weekly, before I DID! And just to clarify something here, if you're a big sister reading this, remember to read the fine print on your contract when signing up for the job in looking out for your baby sister's interests and well-being. You'll discover that it says in the tiniest of font, that your wardrobe automictically becomes mutual property. Oh, I'm sorry, did you miss that rule? Yeah, my big sister did too. You may smile, but to be honest, you'd be astounded to hear all the strategic ways I came up with to get out the front door so my sister didn't see me ~~stealing~~, no, scrub that, *borrowing* her clothes. My stealth-like skills as a kid would have gotten me a job in the central intelligence agency if I'd have been much older.

Honest to God.

Thankfully, my sister was so preoccupied with watching television, that she rarely noticed her clothes missing before I could sneak into her bedroom and put them back in her wardrobe. However, the day finally came when my hidden, devious ways were unmasked by my sister as she pitched her story of complaints to our parents. Needless to say, they sided with my sister, and a padlock was swiftly attached to her bedroom door, and she was given the only key. My sister's smile was as smug and mischievous as the Cheshire Cat's grin.[14] *'Yeah, those are the rules now, baby sister. And you can ONLY come into my room by invitation. Got it!'* Hmm, sometimes being the baby in the family isn't that much fun.

'Moses knows what you mean,' pipes in Miriam as she stands up and brushes down the crumbs from the crusty roll she's been munching on. Remember way back in Exodus chapter 4, when Moses is at the burning bush and he admits to God that he is not a talented speaker? Remember God suggested Aaron to be the spokesperson for him? 'Please, Lord, I beg you to send Your message through someone else, anyone else... How about your brother—Aaron the Levite? I know he speaks eloquently.'[15] Aaron certainly had a way with words that gave a clear, strong message he was a leader who expressed himself well and now his privileged position of high priest came with a whole new wardrobe that resounded and reverberated God's relationship with His people.[16] Let's pick up the story in Exodus chapter 28.

'In order to reflect the glory and beauty of their office, create sacred garments for your brother, Aaron. Talk with all the skilled workers—those whom I have gifted with talent and the spirit of wisdom—and instruct them to create distinct garments that set Aaron apart from others whenever he is serving Me as priest. Here are the ceremonial garments they need to make: a breast piece, a special vest, a robe, a checkered tunic, a turban, and a sash. The craftsmen are to make these sacred items for Aaron your brother and his sons to wear when they come before Me in priestly service... keep the Urim and Thummim in a special pouch on the front of the breast piece of judgement. Aaron must wear these two objects over his heart whenever he enters My presence. This way he will always have with him a way to know My will and make *sound* decisions for the people of Israel... as for the rest of Aaron's sons, make tunics, sashes, and special caps to reflect the glory and beauty of their office. When they serve as priests, dress Aaron, your brother, and his sons in these ceremonial garments; anoint them, ordain them, and consecrate them. Furnish them with linen undergarments, so that they are covered from their waists to their thighs. Aaron and his sons are to put them on whenever they go into the congregation tent or go near the altar to minister in the holy place. They must do this so that they don't incur guilt and die. This directive stands forever for Aaron and all those who come after him.'[17] Aaron literally wore the story of how God's provision and guidance brought the Israelites through difficult times, so they could rise up from the ashes of their past. When the day would finally come for Aaron to leave this earth, his garments would then be passed down and passed on to one of his sons who would succeed him as high priest.[18] His wardrobe became the next generation's wardrobe, and in regard to my underhanded, calculating ways in ~~stealing~~, erm, *borrowing* my big sister's clothes, this wardrobe was shared, appointed, and blessed. Seeing as Miriam was the big sister to two younger brothers, she didn't have to contend with what my sister had to go through regarding her clothes. However, the whole 'your wardrobe is my wardrobe' thought could be carried into Moses and Aaron's relationship. I may be grasping at straws, but just hear me out on this one.

Silence is Golden

My misdeeds in wearing my sister's clothes when I was young all came about while she was preoccupied with something else. Perhaps if I'd have taken a good, hard look in my sister's wardrobe mirror while trying on her brand-new American Football, Miami Dolphins sweatshirt, I would have seen that cover-ups and blaming someone else for my actions wasn't going justify why I was doing something wrong. Although Aaron was clothed in the story of God's relationship with His people, even though Aaron's ceremonial wardrobe reflected God's way of doing things, he failed to take a good, hard look in the mirror at his wardrobe attire while Moses was preoccupied up on Mount Sinai. 'When the people realised Moses was taking a long time to return from his trek up the mountain, they got together and approached Aaron. 'We have no idea what happened to this fellow Moses who brought us out of the land of Egypt. He left you in charge, so get up and make us gods who will lead us from here.'[19] At this point, Aaron should have silenced their pitch and gone through his priestly wardrobe story one garment at a time, mirroring the moments where God redeemed and rescued them from their bondage until it was ringing in the Israelites' ears. However, Aaron's song only reflected his own self-preservation and people-pleasing story instead of reflecting God's story of rescue. Brené Brown pitches in and offers some sound advice, saying that in hard moments, if we choose courage over comfort this is when we *practice* our values rather than just *professing* them[20] because courage doesn't 'choose silence over what is right.'[20] (emphasis mine). For a warrior, rising above the status quo will often come with uncomfortable moments and this is where we'll have to choose whether we're going to be bold and courageous in voicing our values and beliefs or allow them to be silenced by the crowd.

The enemy loves to mute a warrior's song into silence because silence is golden as far as the devil is concerned. In the meantime, Aaron continues to compromise in his leadership. "I want you to bring me the gold earrings your wives, sons, and daughters are wearing. So, everyone took out their gold earrings and handed them over to Aaron. He collected the gold they brought and used a tool to fashion an idol in the shape of a calf. When the people saw the calf Aaron made, they were elated. (People seeing the calf) "Israel, these are your gods—the ones who led you out of the land of Egypt." When Aaron saw how the people responded, he built an altar in front of the golden calf.'[21] Hold on. *These are your gods—the ones who led you out of the land of Egypt?!* I know, this part of the story just leaves me speechless. For the pitch of your song to make the enemy's ears pop, there are three things in this passage we need to be aware of. Believe me, when you hear them, you'll understand what happens when a weak leader starts heading down the perilous path of compromise, and it's something we warriors need to be attentive and all ears to.

Firstly, for Aaron to fashion and form a golden calf so the people had something to worship was as careless as it was faulty. But the unacceptable action was that he approved God's people to say that the golden calf was the god who led them out of Egypt. This just caused God's anger to ignite. Secondly, remember Aaron asked the people to bring the gold earrings of the sons and daughters? Alarm bells start ringing for me because the ordered, detailed story of God's deliverance of His people from the bondage of Egypt was being blended with compromise. This new trade-off story was now being listened to by the next generation and Aaron's misguided leadership had the dangerous potential of igniting something other than God's will that could eventually send the sons and daughters back into slavery. Perhaps a different kind of slavery than the shackles and chains that Pharaoh put them in, but slavery none the less. As Lisa Bevere points out, 'an idol is anything that you give your strength to or draw your strength from... compromise (is) losing their voices and their freedom of movement.'[22] Nowadays, we don't form and fashion golden calves, however, we can create idols when we put something, anything above God, thus making a deal with the devil. Thirdly, Aaron saw how the people responded, so he built an altar in front of the golden calf. A weak leader's deepest fear is losing their position and title if they speak out truth in love. Appeasing and pacifying the crowd by giving what they want is key to a weak leader keeping their place. Remember Aaron's priestly garments had the Urim and Thummim, the two objects that were placed over his heart whenever he entered into God's presence so that he will always have with him a way to know God's will and make *sound* decisions for the people of Israel? Yeah, Aaron's weak leadership actions are only fuelled by fear and self-preservation and the enemy is all too happy to fan those flames.

So, to rub salt into the gaping wound, Aaron organises a feast for the *god* who brought them out of Egypt, and at this point, God tells Moses what's going on. Scripture doesn't go into detail, and like I said, I could be clutching at straws, but even though on the outside Aaron wore the priestly garments that reflected God's heart, his weak leadership skills were telling a different story. Moses wore a wardrobe that reflected the wardrobe the apostle Paul speaks about in Colossians 12-17. 'So, chosen by God for this new life of love, dress in a wardrobe God picked out for you: compassion, kindness, humility, quiet strength, discipline. Be even-tempered, content with second place, quick to forgive an offense. Forgive as quickly and completely as the Master forgave you. And regardless of what else you put on, wear love. It's your basic, all-purpose garment. Never be without it.'[23]

Who is the Song For?

To set the record straight, Moses needed to confront his older brother and get the Israelites back to singing the same tune. 'Go back down the mountain immediately, because your people whom you led out of Egypt have corrupted themselves. They have quickly abandoned the way of life I require of them. They have fashioned a calf out of gold, bowed down to it, and offered it sacrifices. They are even crediting My work to that detestable idol, saying, 'Israel, these are your gods—the ones who brought you out of the land of Egypt... leave Me alone so that My anger can flare up and destroy them.'[24] Thankfully, Moses talks God out of annihilating the Israelites and heads back down the mountain quick smart. 'As they neared the camp, Joshua heard the commotion and the people shouting. (To Moses) "It is not the sound of victory, and it's not the sound of defeat, but I do hear singing and celebration." As soon as Moses arrived at the camp, he saw the calf and the revelry around it. His anger flared... He took down the calf they had made and burned it. "How could you lead these people into such a heinous sin? What did they do to you?" (Aaron) "Control your anger, my master. You know these people. You know how evil they can be... so, I told them, "If you are wearing any gold, take it off." So, they gave me all their gold and I just tossed it into the fire, and out came this calf!'[25] Aaron, please come on, '*I just tossed all the gold into the fire and out came a calf*' doesn't wash with a warrior like Moses, so just stop with the excuses. Okay? Compromise leads to forming and fashioning a song that isn't a song of victory, or the sound of defeat, but a song that celebrates the idols we worship, and the sad truth is that Aaron's weak leadership was a leveraging point for his big sister, Miriam to take advantage of.

Endnotes: Chapter Fifteen

Ref 1   Funny Sister Quotes: southernliving.com.

Ref 2   Website: aulart.com 'Understanding the importance of pitch in music.'

Ref 3   Exodus 24:3. Ecclesia Bible Society. 2012. *The Voice Bible: Step into the Story of Scripture.* Nashville: Thomas Nelson.

Ref 4   Exodus 25:8. Ecclesia Bible Society. 2012. *The Voice Bible: Step into the Story of Scripture.* Nashville: Thomas Nelson.

Ref 5   Walton, John H, Victor Harold Matthews, and Mark William Chavalas. 2000.*The IVP Bible Background Commentary Old Testament.* Downers Grove, III. Intervarsity Press.

Ref 6   Exodus 28:1-3. Ecclesia Bible Society. 2012. *The Voice Bible: Step into the Story of Scripture.* Nashville: Thomas Nelson.

Ref 7   Exodus 28, Biblical commentary. Ecclesia Bible Society. 2012. *The Voice Bible: Step into the Story of Scripture.* Nashville: Thomas Nelson.

Ref 8   thesaurus.com

Ref 9   1 Peter 2:9. Ecclesia Bible Society. 2012. *The Voice Bible: Step into the Story of Scripture.* Nashville: Thomas Nelson.

Ref 10   Austin, Jill. 2007. *Dancing with Destiny: Awaken your heart to dream, to love, to war.* Chosen Books Publishing.

Ref 11   Science.howstuffworks.com Jun 9, 2023.

Ref 12   James 4:7. Ecclesia Bible Society. 2012. *The Voice Bible: Step into the Story of Scripture.* Nashville: Thomas Nelson.

Ref 13   James 4:7. *Amplified Holy Compact Bible: Captures the Full Meaning behind the Original Greek and Hebrew.* 2015. Grand Rapids, Michigan: Zondervan.

Ref 14   Wikipedia 'Cheshire Cat' created by Lewis Carroll

Ref 15   Exodus 4:14. Ecclesia Bible Society. 2012. *The Voice Bible: Step into the Story of Scripture.* Nashville: Thomas Nelson.

Ref 16   Biblical commentary of Exodus 28. Ecclesia Bible Society. 2012. *The Voice Bible: Step into the Story of Scripture.* Nashville: Thomas Nelson.

Ref 17   Exodus 28:2-4, Exodus 28:30, Exodus 28:40-43. Ecclesia Bible Society. 2012. *The Voice Bible: Step into the Story of Scripture.* Nashville: Thomas Nelson.

Ref 18   Exodus 29:29. Ecclesia Bible Society. 2012. *The Voice Bible: Step into the Story of Scripture.* Nashville: Thomas Nelson.

Ref 19   Exodus 32:2. Ecclesia Bible Society. 2012. *The Voice Bible: Step into the Story of Scripture.* Nashville: Thomas Nelson.

Ref 20   Brown, Brené. 2018. *Dare to lead*: Brave Work. Tough Conversations. Whole Hearts. New York: Random House.

Ref 21   Exodus 32:2-5. Ecclesia Bible Society. 2012. *The Voice Bible: Step into the Story of Scripture.* Nashville: Thomas Nelson.

Ref 22   Bevere, Lisa. 2016. *Without Rival: Embrace Your Identity and Purpose in an Age of Confusion and Comparison.* Baker Books.

Ref 23   Colossians 3:12-14: Peterson, Eugene H. 1995. *The Message Bible.* Colorado Springs,   Co: Navpress.

Ref 24   Exodus 32: 7-10. Ecclesia Bible Society. 2012. *The Voice Bible: Step into the Story of Scripture.* Nashville: Thomas Nelson.

Ref 25   Exodus 32: 17-24. Ecclesia Bible Society. 2012. *The Voice Bible: Step into the Story of Scripture.* Nashville: Thomas Nelson.

CHAPTER SIXTEEN

Singing the Blues

'When I'm singing the blues, I'm singing life.'[1]
ETTA JAMES

Sensing the weight of Miriam's grief in the retelling of the golden calf incident clearly reveals how this dark, soot-covered moment shackled the Israelites feet in their rising, causing them to fall flat on their faces. How was Moses going to sort out this mess and mend the Israelites fractured relationship with God? They'd become a joke to their enemies and Moses realised their rebellion wasn't going escape God's disciplinary action. Sure, the Israelites had left Egypt behind them, however, Moses quickly identified the stamp etched into that golden calf had Egyptian idol worship written all over it. 'He stood at the camp's entrance and shouted to them. "If you are on the side of the Eternal One, stand over here with me!" All the Levites gathered around him. (To the Levites) "This is the message of the Eternal One, Israel's true God: 'Every one of you strap on your sword and move throughout the entire camp. Kill your brother, friend, and neighbour.'" The Levites did exactly as Moses told them to do, and about 3,000 men were killed that day.'[2] See how compromise leads to rebellion and rebellion leads to division which leads to an uprising rather than a rising? I'm quite sure when Aaron tossed all that gold into the fire, he wasn't banking on 3,000 men losing their lives because of his careless actions. I'll give full credit to Moses' warrior attitude in this situation because he doesn't decide to hush-up, sit on, and smother this wrongdoing of idol worship. He doesn't choose to muffle and dampen the sound of the people's sin because he wants everyone to like him and tell him what a great guy he is. No, he calls the sin out because he's aware their covenant relationship with God needs to be redeemed so they can move onwards and upwards. 'You are guilty of a great sin. Now I am going back to the Eternal One, and I hope to make atonement for your wickedness.'[3] Moses decides he is going to take full responsibly and make amends with God by standing in the gap for the people. 'These people are guilty of a great sin against You. They fashioned gods out of gold for themselves. If You will only forgive their sin, but if You do not, then erase me from the book You have written.'[4] Wait, you're telling me that Moses' love for the Israelites meant that he was willing to be separated, cursed, and blotted out of God's book by taking on the full punishment of the people's sin just to save them all?[5]

Yeah, sacrificial love does that.

Something had changed, something had shifted on the inside of Moses, as this is the same guy who had made a song and dance at the burning bush, pleading, and battling with God as to why He must choose someone else because Moses felt he wasn't the right person for the job in leading the Israelites out of Egypt. Take your sandals off, dear warrior, as this is truly holy ground.

This sacred, transitional moment is possibly Moses' greatest growth in his warrior journey, as he decided to believe that God had indeed called him and commissioned him to stand in the gap so others would be saved. I'm delighted to say that God wasn't going to allow Moses to take the hit for his brother's mistake. But God did send a plague on all the people as punishment because 'they had bowed down and sacrificed to the calf Aaron had made.'[6] No excuses this time, Aaron had been called out. And yet, this situation had reignited the warrior within Moses and his song was rising to a whole other level. The ammunition for the follow-up shot was Moses' belief in himself. A God-confidence, not a self-confidence in leading the people, and as Jessica Brody advises, 'believing in yourself is sometimes the only weapon you'll need.'[7] Now that thought is going to boost your confidence and get you up out of the comfort zone of staying in those ashes for sure! Moses had possibly never tapped into his inner warrior as much as he did in this moment, and he was ready to sing a different tune. Listen, dear warrior, it will do us no good to keep singing the blues and sitting in the ashes when things go pear-shaped. We need to dust ourselves off, get back in the fight, and take ownership and responsibility for our actions and decisions instead of blaming everyone else as to why things happened the way they did. And in doing so, we help others to find the freedom and courage to rise up too.[8]

Three-Stranded Cord

This is where the next two elements in the follow-up shot come into play. The timbre (pronounced tam-ber) and the dynamics each play a part in our song rising.[9] When the exact same melody is played by either a human voice or an instrument you can tell them apart by the timbre.[9] The sound from a person's voice could be described as harsh, piercing, shrill, throaty, velvety, or whispered.[9] With an instrument, the volume all depends on whether it is struck soft or hard as this changes the intensity of the sound after the attack.[9] Dynamics is another word for volume and it is the level of volume the sound needs to make as the piece of music or song is performed.[9] After the rift between God and His people was resolved, God instructed Moses to cut two stone tablets so God's laws that made up the covenant were loud and clear to each one of the Israelites. 'In all Moses was with the Eternal One for 40 days and 40 nights. He fasted the entire time— no food or water. He wrote down the Ten Directives, the essential words of the covenant, on the two stone tablets.[10] I know we're spending a fair amount of time on the golden calf incident, but I feel it's important to tune into what we can learn through the pain of singing the blues. It seems the three warriors had a weak link in the chain of command and as the saying goes, 'you're only as strong as your weakest link.' In Ecclesiastes 4:12, King Solomon reminds us that 'a cord of three strands is not quickly broken'[11] and the actions of Aaron could well be the opening the enemy was waiting for so he could divide and conquer, breaking the three-strand cord that connected these three warrior leaders.

Sing Higher, Sing Louder

The trajectory of your warrior's journey should always be moving in an upwards direction, however, there are inevitable moments where we will fall flat on our faces in our rising as we reach altitudes, we never dreamed possible. To use the quote of Victor Kiam, 'Even when you fall on your face, you're still moving forward'[12] this thought helps warriors to keep going so it stops the paralysing effect of blaming the devil for everything that goes wrong. Don't misunderstand me, our enemy is just as relentlessly committed to his schemes in diverting our flight attempts up out of the ashes as he ever was, fulfilling his dirty dealings one masterful deception at a time, making sure all our disappointments dull the spark so the warrior within never becomes reignited. As the apostle Paul writes to the Corinthians, we are not naïve enough to fall prey to his schemes.[13] For warriors to be truly free, we need stop fooling ourselves, stop blaming the devil for everything and confess our sins. As 1 John 1:5-9 says, 'God is pure light, undimmed by darkness of any kind. If we say we have an intimate connection with the Father, but we continue stumbling around in darkness, then we are lying because we do not live according to truth. If we walk step-by-step in the light, where the Father is, then we are ultimately connected to each other through the sacrifice of Jesus His Son. His blood purifies us from all our sins. If we go around bragging, "We have no sin," then we are fooling ourselves and are strangers to the truth. But if we own up to our sins, God shows that He is faithful and just by forgiving us of our sins and purifying us from the pollution.'[14]

We tend to not use the word *sin* anymore in polite church circles just in case we sound too judgemental, but we're just kidding ourselves if we don't call it out for what it is. There is no way around, over, or under it, sin and the pain that comes from it needs to be dealt with, otherwise it pollutes and chokes your song. Even in a natural sense, research has shown that pollution, especially noise pollution in urban areas, affect a bird's song, and some species need to sing at a higher frequency to ensure they are heard.[15] To stop sin's pollution getting onto our flight feathers, we need to come clean with our sin and repent of it. Perhaps all this talk of sin may be ruffling a few Phoenix feathers, however, if we're going to rise up into all God has for us, we can't pretend that we have no part of sin and it's all the devil's fault. In Psalm 32, David's contemplative song confesses his sin to God, and he quickly discovers through his confession that God is indeed his safe hiding place and He keeps him out of trouble, enveloping David with songs that remind him he is free.[16] We can't keep sinning and then aiming cheap follow-up shots at the devil, taking none of the responsibility for our own actions. We need our shots to be clean and confess our sin to God on the regular, as this is the song that keeps reminding warriors that their freedom was brought at great cost.

Beware of Fishing Lines

As Miriam leads us to a higher altitude in our warrior journey, you've found that your breath has become shorter, you feel dizzy and lethargic as each one of the steps in your rising has just become so much harder. The fear of not being able to make it, as the backpack you're carrying feels like there is now an iron anvil in it, gives you the sense that you're just not good enough to rise up into a warrior status because your past keeps you singing the blues, urging you to find a safe place to hide, somewhere you can retreat because you know you'll find the comfort you crave for in that small space as you slowly pick at the scars because you're feeling the shame from your mistakes. You wonder if you'll ever be free from the ashes of the past. Surely there is an easier way to rise up to become a warrior than this steep climb. Be careful, dear warrior, don't fall for it, as this is where the enemy is always fishing for your demise as he entangles and ties around your shame-filled thinking. Ever seen a bird get trapped in a fishing line? At first, the fine line was invisible to the bird as it searched for food, until it was too late, and it became entangled as the fishing line wrapped itself around the helpless bird's flight wings and around its neck. Bird rescuers know that 'If birds become entangled they are essentially trapped and cannot free themselves without assistance. They are prevented from flying, walking, feeding, and avoiding predators.'[17] Firebirds need reminding that the enemy never changes his tactics, as Adam and Eve can attest to. Their fall from grace came when the devil offered them a quick-fix detour in the journey of their rising. Believing the sly old snake was for them, they took a large bite and swallowed that lie, hook, line, and sinker. Hanna E. Farwell suggests that the devil is always 'trying to persuade humankind to take the easy route... (as) most sins are committed by meeting legitimate needs in illegitimate ways.'[18] God is cheering you on to become a warrior, however, He wants you to go on the up and up correctly, as it isn't just the altitude that starts changing as we rise but our attitude starts to change when we realise we can never free ourselves from sin. However, Jesus paid the ultimate price for us to rise up from the ashes of sin and fly into our freedom as His scars remind us we need to stop singing the blues and start humming a different tune. Miriam asks you to think back to the moment you decided to stop running in your forest of pain, the moment you found that little cabin in the clearing. She wants you to remember the window boxes on each side of the narrow door as you entered the little cabin, and she reminds you of all the different coloured flowers that represented the great cloud of witnesses that have gone before us. Miriam recites Hebrews 12:1 as you think about those flowers while we're taking the last few steps to the summit. 'So, since we stand surrounded by all those who have gone before, an enormous cloud of witnesses, let us drop every extra weight, every sin that clings to us and slackens our pace, and let us run with endurance the long race set before us.'[19] As you peer over the summit you discover there is a whole carpet of different coloured flowers spread out before you. Miriam turns to you and says, 'Each flower represents a warrior who has gone before you, and it was their faith that convinced them to carry on, even when their journey became hard, even when they didn't see their promises come to pass. They are cheering you on, dear warrior.' And with that thought, it seems the backpack you've been carrying up this mountain has suddenly become a whole lot lighter.

Endnotes: Chapter Sixteen

Ref 1   Quote: quotement.com. 210 Best Singing Quotes To Make You Sing Your Heart Out. by Kristen Hill

Ref 2   Exodus 32:26-28: Ecclesia Bible Society. 2012. *The Voice Bible: Step into the Story of Scripture.* Nashville: Thomas Nelson.

Ref 3   Exodus 32:30: Ecclesia Bible Society. 2012. *The Voice Bible: Step into the Story of Scripture.* Nashville: Thomas Nelson.

Ref 4   Exodus 32:31-32: Ecclesia Bible Society. 2012. *The Voice Bible: Step into the Story of Scripture.* Nashville: Thomas Nelson.

Ref 5   Biblical commentary on Exodus 32. Syswerda, Jean, and Faith Organization.2001. NIV Women of Faith Study Bible: New International Version. Grand Rapids, Mich.: Zondervan.

Ref 6   Exodus 32:35: Ecclesia Bible Society. 2012. *The Voice Bible: Step into the Story of Scripture.* Nashville: Thomas Nelson.

Ref 7   Brody, Jessica. 2018. *Save the Cat! Writes a Novel : The Last Book on Novel Writing You'll Ever Need.* Berkeley, California: Ten Speed Press.

Ref 8   Erwin Raphael McManus. 2019. *The Way Of The Warrior: An Ancient Path To Inner Peace.* New York: Waterbrook.

Ref 9   Website: kaitlinbove.com/elements-of-music

Ref 10   Exodus 34:28: Ecclesia Bible Society. 2012. *The Voice Bible: Step into the Story of Scripture.* Nashville: Thomas Nelson.

Ref 11   Ecclesiastes 4:12: *Amplified Holy Compact Bible: Captures the Full Meaning behind the Original Greek and Hebrew.* 2015. Grand Rapids, Michigan: Zondervan.

Ref 12   BrainyQuote.Com

Ref 13   2 Corinthians 2:11: Ecclesia Bible Society. 2012. *The Voice Bible: Step into the Story of Scripture.* Nashville: Thomas Nelson.

Ref 14   1 John 1:5-9: Ecclesia Bible Society. 2012. *The Voice Bible: Step into the Story of Scripture.* Nashville: Thomas Nelson.

Ref 15   Website:bto.org 'Birds and pollution—a masterclass'. Nina O' Hanlon

Ref 16   Psalm 32:7: Ecclesia Bible Society. 2012. *The Voice Bible: Step into the Story of Scripture.* Nashville: Thomas Nelson.

Ref 17   Website: birdmonitors.com Chicago Bird Collision Monitors—CBCM (Migratory bird rescue and protection)

Ref 18   Farwell, Hanna. 2010. *The Sword and the Tamborine: Becoming a Warrior Through Worship.* Destiny Image Publishers.

Ref 19   Hebrews 12:1: Ecclesia Bible Society. 2012. *The Voice Bible: Step into the Story of Scripture.* Nashville: Thomas Nelson.

CHAPTER SEVENTEEN

Finding Our Way

*'But what song will you sing when your soul gets set free?
I think it will be something true and beautiful '*[1]
DONALD MILLER

We are going to unpack the final two elements of our song, now that you have understood why the tempo, rhythm, pitch, timbre, and dynamics all help to create a powerful follow-up shot you can aim straight into the enemy's camp, time and time again. But before we add the melody and harmony and put the finishing touches to our song, I just want to take a moment to say something here. The reason why we have journeyed steadily and deliberately through each one of the seven elements of our follow-up shot is for the simple fact that the devil isn't all that impressed with wannabe warriors. The reality is, that those type of heroes come in all guns blazing, firing their cheap shots because they like the *sound* of becoming a warrior. And as things go, they certainly do look very impressive. However, these social climbers are only in it for themselves as they do their best to avoid the discomfort and difficulty of getting their hands dirty because taking back territory from the enemy's camp is sometimes a thankless task. You struggle to find a wannabe warrior when we're in the fray of conflict and confrontation, feeling out of our depth and we're up to our necks in it, as these situations tend to thin out the crowd of keen, hopeful wannabes because they suddenly realise that success in God's kingdom is completely different to what the world deems success. A true warrior doesn't spend too much time thinking about self-preservation and self-promotion because, as I have mentioned at the start of our journey, the warrior is the one who is willing to sacrifice themselves for others. Not only that, but all the glory, yes, that's *all the glory*, goes to God and not to themselves.

Be that as it may, I do not believe this describes you because if you have made it this far in our journey then you're clearly no wannabe warrior. If you're still ready to rise up from the ashes, regardless of how much heat comes from the flames of affliction, hardship, pain, and difficulty, then you have discovered that reigniting the warrior within is not for the faint of heart. It can be a lonesome, solitary road at times as warriors face many trials and battles in being misunderstood and misinterpreted by others. So, seeing as we're having a candid moment here on this mountain top as Miriam lets you soak in the awe and beauty of the carpet of flowers that represent the great cloud of warrior witnesses who have learned to rise before you, let me be clear in the fact that your follow-up shot is as necessary as it is needed. However, what rattles and shakes the enemy's camp more than anything is the authenticity of a true warrior whose faith has been tested in the fire. You see, the legend of the Phoenix all pivots on one aspect—its rising. I'm getting ahead of myself, but I feel you need a little encouraging pep talk in this pivotal, pinnacle moment of your rising, for it is in the resurrection part of the narrative where the firebird discovers its power because it has found a way out of the ashes. In 1 Peter 1:4-7, Peter talks about authentic faith. 'We are reborn into a perfect inheritance that can never perish, never be defiled, and never diminish. It is promised and preserved forever in the heavenly realm for you! Through our faith, the mighty power of God constantly guards us until our *full* salvation is ready to be revealed in the last time. May the thought of this cause you to jump for joy, even though lately you've had to put up with the grief of many trials. But these only reveal the sterling core of your faith, which is far more valuable than gold that perishes, for even gold is refined by fire. *Your authentic faith* will result in even more praise, glory, and honour when Jesus the Anointed One is revealed.'[2] God is calling out His legitimate, bona fide warriors to tap into His resurrection power so they can rise up from the ashes of their past and walk right through the refining flames. This part of your story is where God's authoritative stamp of His kingdom approval makes your victory song so annoyingly persistent that the devil won't be able to get the tune out of his head.

The Backbone to Your Song

Did you know that the melody is known as the backbone because it guides and supports a song? I like that. Also, melody is the most recognisable part of a song as the sequence of sounds are sometimes played at a higher pitch.[3] I like that too. The enemy can quickly identify and recognise a follow-up shot that has been fired with some backbone, on the grounds that the sequence of familiar sounds have been raised with a few battle cries of hallelujahs. The devil knows a real warrior when he sees one and this is why he's always trying to undermine our God-given authority. His aim is for us to back down or back out of our rising, so we never string the sequence of sounds together, helping us to walk in the authority and strength God has given to us. I have little doubt in my own warrior journey, that whenever I chose to trust God and decided to step into my God-given authority as a leader, the enemy often sent someone to try and intimidate me in the hope my wings started to cramp up, causing me to drawback to the point of disappearing into the ashes altogether. Because I had no backbone to my song, no recognisable sequence of sounds in my follow-up shot, the devil's scare tactics normally succeeded in making sure I stayed quiet, stayed small, and stayed invisible, as he knew that I knew, if I did decide to be bold and courageous then my actions would have dire consequences. So, I was convinced that speaking up about things that didn't sit right with me and the injustice surrounding certain issues would just make everyone else feel very uncomfortable and then they possibly wouldn't like me anymore. And believe me, no people-pleasing, good girl was ever going to allow *that* to happen.

Intimidation is the coercion that threatens your safety in your rising, and as John Bevere observed, the tactic of intimidation designed by the enemy is to swipe your God-given authority right from under your nose. Like John, there was a time when I was 'knocked out of my position of authority so that the gift of God is quenched'[4] and I found that whenever I did muster enough courage to speak out about something that didn't feel right, my rising suddenly came to an abrupt end and I'd find myself straight back down in those ashes quick smart. It seemed no matter how hard I tried to rise up, something in my song was missing. Somehow, no matter how much I flapped my wings, regardless of how much straining and striving I did, I never got past a certain point. For some reason I always ended up sliding miserably back down into the ash pile, feeling that familiar feeling I was missing out on something God had asked me to boldly ascend into. This endless cycle left me feeling depleted, frustrated, and resentful.

Rest assured, my follow-up shot has gained some backbone over the years as I've slowly let God into the most painful parts of my past so He could work on my fears and insecurities, teaching me to rise up into the responsibility He had entrusted me with and to push past the points I found the intimidation tactics of the enemy were designed to make me quit. Hiding and staying small isn't what warriors were made for, and I'm so grateful that God didn't shake His head and roll His eyes as He watched my doubts, worries, fears, and insecurities get the better of me. He never condemned me as I kept banging my head on the glass ceiling of my rising, the ceiling made from my own self-imposed limitations and say, 'Oh, for goodness' sake! Get some backbone into that song of yours, Wendy! Come on girl, you've got to suck it up, rise up, and soldier on!' I think, if we believe God behaves like a drill sergeant with us every time, we let the intimidation tactics of the enemy get the better of us, then we're missing the whole point as to why God asks us to rise up and become a warrior. Why would God counteract intimidation tactics with intimidation tactics, right? The thing is, we read in our Bibles how God will never leave us in the ashes. I mean sure, we get that part of the whole warrior rising process. In fact, we've got that part of the promise paid for and in the bag, it's done and dusted as far as we're concerned. And yet, where we get stuck and have difficulty grasping is the truthful fact that God doesn't abandon us in the fire of our transition either, because as the melody to our follow-up shot is being formed, *He is* the backbone that guides and supports us through the transformation process. And when that revelation seeps into our warrior thick skull, we can rise past the intimidation scare campaign of the enemy's plan of attack.

Remember Moses went from being completely intimidated by the power and authority of Pharaoh, to a willing warrior who was ready to sacrifice himself by taking on the full punishment of the people's sin so they would all be saved because Aaron made a huge mistake in making the golden calf. Can you see the intimidation flames trying to push Moses back down into those ashes? However, Moses heard the melody of the call to move beyond his comfort zone and limitations, using the idol worshipping opportunity to grow and develop some backbone into his song. Take note and recognise the specific parts in your rising where the enemy uses his intimidation tactics to scare you into retreat. I can guarantee you'll be able to connect the dots. Perhaps you need to do something? Maybe you need to speak up about something? What part gets the devil rattled in your rising?

To be honest, I have always been cautious in speaking out about things and of course, wisdom is needed. However, as I've followed God's guidance and found my way through the flames in my rising, I've realised that He is looking for someone who speaks up and puts a stop to injustice and lies. It says in Isaiah 59 that God is looking for intercessors who aren't afraid to stand in the gap. 'God looked long and hard, but there wasn't a single person who tried to put a stop to the injustice and lies. So, God took action. His own strong arm reached out and brought salvation. His own righteousness—good and pure—sustained Him. But God's equipment was that of no ordinary warrior: He strapped on righteousness as His breastplate and put on the helmet of salvation. Wrapped in vengeance for clothing and passion as a cloak, God prepared for war... this is My covenant promise to them: my Spirit which rests on and moves in you, and My words, which I have placed within you, will continue to be spoken among you and move you to action. And not only you, but it will be for your children and their children too. And so on through the generations for all time.'[5] Oh yes! I like the sound of this passage because warriors are all for legacy. Know this, dear firebird, God's Spirit moves in you and His words placed within you will move you to action because His breastplate of righteousness and helmet of salvation lets the enemy know that you're no ordinary warrior.

As I have boldly spoken out about the things that are not God's way of doing things, and sometimes done it with my heart racing and my knees shaking, I have gained the respect of others that would not necessarily had been given to me if I hadn't spoken out about something. Sometimes warriors have to lean into the uncomfortableness and become the intercessor who speaks up for the oppressed, the marginalised, and the voiceless.

Blend of Sounds

Harmony is different to the melody as it is a blend of sounds that are played together in a song.[6] When the overcomers rise together in unity, the enemy hears the harmony of our follow-up shot because his number one strategy is to divide and conquer. Although the warrior journey can be isolated and lonely at times as you find your way through the flames, moving beyond the intimidation tactics of the enemy as you learn to lean into a 'holy trust'[7] with God, we still need the support of others. In Exodus 17, the Israelites had to battle it out with the soldiers of Amalek. 'While the Israelites were camped at Rephidim, soldiers of Amalek came and attacked them. Moses called for a young leader named Joshua.'[8] *Spoiler alert* this is the same Joshua who would eventually succeed in Moses' leadership. Moses was clearly training and mentoring Joshua in the ways of the warrior because he says to him, 'Select some of our best men, and go fight against the soldiers of Amalek. Tomorrow I will stand at the crest of that hill overlooking the battlefield with God's staff in my hand.' Joshua did exactly as Moses had instructed him to do. He gathered the strongest men he could find and fought against the soldiers of Amalek. Meanwhile, Moses, Aaron, and Hur climbed to the top of the hill. It happened that whenever Moses raised his hand, the battle went well for Israel; but whenever he lowered his hand to rest, Amalek began to win. When Moses became too tired to hold his hands up any longer, Aaron and Hur took a stone and sat down on it. Then both men stood beside Moses, one on each side, holding his hands up and keeping them steady until sunset. In the end, Joshua and the men of Israel defeated Amalek and his soldiers with the sword... then Moses constructed an altar and called it "The Eternal is My Battle Flag."'[9] Biblical commentary suggests that Egyptian texts mention the uplifted arms of Pharaoh as it was seen as protection in battles as well as a signal to attack.[10] I love the imaginary of Aaron and Hur standing beside Moses, one on each side of him so they could hold up his arms to keep him steady. Doesn't this theme remind you of the delivery stool where Shiphrah and Puah, the two midwives, helped Jochebed with the birth of her son? And like the three women that helped to deliver a deliverer, the three-strand cord was now being formed by three warrior men who needed the Israelites to be delivered from the Amaleks. This pattern of assistance not only affirms warriors are supported either side by others in the natural, but we are also supported supernaturally by Jehovah-nissi. He is our banner over us, our provider, the God who sustains His warriors in the fight.[11] He is also, Jehovah Gibbor, 'The LORD the mighty warrior' who fights on behalf of His people and delivers them from the enemy.[12] Working in harmony is the unity that ties the follow-up shot together as warriors rise up into a great and mighty army of overcomers, encouraging and helping one another, with Jehovah-nissi as the banner over them. Let me be clear, unity doesn't mean we become cookie-cutter warriors on an assembly line, linked together to make a holy huddle. There is no power in that kind of set up. But a blend of sounds, a collective group of warriors, an undivided force for good that lift each other up in the heat of battle because Jehovah Gibbor fights *with* them and *for* them is what makes the enemy sweat.

Smoothing the Rough Edges

We seem to have gone off on a bit of a tangent with Moses, which is easy to do in the Exodus story. However, we need to find our way back to Miriam's role and the part she played. Her youngest brother was no doubt a biblical giant when it came to reigniting the warrior within, but if we're going to talk about support from others, and the melody and harmony that make up the final stages of our song, we need Miriam to share some hard-won truths just to smooth out any rough edges on our follow-up shot.

Rough edges? Surly not. Miriam is a legendary warrior! For a few chapters in Exodus, Miriam isn't mentioned until the book of Numbers, and it's a moment in her story that left her isolated and shut out of the community.

Perhaps Miriam's rebellion was birthed in the smouldering ashes of feeling left out, looked over, or the dusty desert life was just taking its toll. Possibly. We shall never know. But one thing is certain, Miriam's part in the whole story was vital to her two brother's important roles. The prophetess Miriam. A tambourine wielding worship warrior whose life of service to God had taught her how to become humble and play the role God had assigned for her are all leadership lessons we can learn from Miriam. And yet, she wasn't without her faults because Miriam learned the hard way that the foundation of relying on God had to be built on trusting in His direction. The small issue of Moses marrying a foreigner quickly became a big issue for Miriam and Aaron. 'While they were at Hazeroth, Miriam and Aaron chastised Moses for marrying a foreign woman—a Cushite (and it was true that he did indeed marry such an African). "Has the Eternal One only spoken through Moses? No, the Eternal has also spoken through us." Now, the Eternal One heard this. For his part, Moses was a uniquely humble fellow, more humble than anyone in the entire world. All of a sudden, the Eternal called the three siblings together. "Come here, you three—Moses, Aaron, and Miriam. Join Me, at the congregation tent." They did. The Eternal One descended in a cloud-column, stood at the tent opening, and summoned just Aaron and Miriam. They came forward.'[13]

I'm just going to pause the story here and take a stab in the dark, but I sense God is about to address this issue that has arisen between the siblings. Miriam was possibly the stronger leader, as the golden calf 'incident' can attest to Aaron being a weak leader.

This could be why Miriam managed to talk Aaron into helping berate their younger brother, Moses. Nothing escapes God's notice, and this questioning of Moses' leadership becomes a costly move for Miriam as she pays dearly for this error because God strikes her down with leprosy. Patrick Lencioni speaks about the peril of avoiding difficult conversations because they are awkward. However, he warns that 'failing to confront people quickly about small issues is a guarantee that they will become big issues.'[14] Clearly, there was a big issue between the warriors. 'The Eternal left, quite angry with Miriam and Aaron. When the cloud lifted from the congregation tent, you could see that Miriam has been stricken with a disfiguring skin condition. Her skin looked white, like snow.[15]

Are We Willing?

Leprosy, or Hansen's disease, is an infection that can lead to damaged nerves, skin, eyes, and respiratory tract. This damage could result in the loss of a person's ability to feel any pain.[16]

In the ancient world, it was referred to as the 'living death' and victims would be treated as though they had died already.[17] To a wounded warrior, losing the ability to not feel the unpleasantness that pain brings sounds like a welcome relief as pain often leaves us feeling ostracized and isolated. I know, I have the scars to prove it. Leadership can be difficult and agonizingly hard at times, but the danger is that as leaders losing the ability to not feel pain stops our built-in alarm system becoming aware that something is going wrong and nullifies our compacity to protect. Samuel R. Chand warns leaders that, 'ignoring pain is leadership leprosy. It may promise the short-term gain of avoiding discomfort, but it has devastating long-term consequences.'[18] Again, I have *those* scars too.

So, how did Miriam go from tambourine waving warrior to looking like death warmed up? Well, she had developed a rebellious spirit, one that was possibly fuelled with the burning embers of jealousy because of her brother's intimate relationship with God, as the crux of the protest was really about God only speaking through Moses. Some say it was to do with Moses marrying a foreign wife, but I believe the underlying current ran deeper than that. Miriam had spent her whole life involved in finding her way through circumstances and trusting God for the outcome no matter how impossible rising up into His promises seemed.

Now her critical and cutting remarks towards Moses revealed a jealous, rebellious spirit that God needed to deal with before the matter was cleared up and they could move on.

'So, Miriam was shut out of the community for seven days, which also meant that the whole group didn't travel until Miriam was brought back in, and they set out again.'[19] I believe, as warrior leaders, we can glean so much wisdom in how God deals with us when we start to develop a wrong attitude just in that one short sentence alone in Numbers 12:15. I find that we can skip past, gloss over, and miss the fact that God wouldn't allow anyone else in the community to move on until Miriam went through the process of an attitude change. Perhaps, in this passage, God is trying to show us something here and we warriors need to sit up and pay attention.

See, the trouble with Christian circles is that we always want to skip past, gloss over, and move on as quickly and as smoothly as possible with people's 'issues' because, hey, we have a Promised Land to get to, right? As a result, on the outside our appearance may have all the hallmarks of a warrior, with our polished breastplate, sharpened sword, and the grit and determination that could intimidate a grizzly bear into retreating. Oh yes, we've got this warrior gig down pat. However, as John C. Maxwell warns, 'a neglected and underdeveloped attitude are the hidden areas in our personal lives that need to be dealt with. It's not just a case of can we change, it whether we are *willing*.'[20] Thankfully, Moses and Aaron pleaded with God to heal their big sister and God did indeed heal Miriam after seven days of thinking about her way of looking at things. Sure, the outward signs of leprosy were gone, and Miriam's body was back to normal, and yet, something had possibly changed within Miriam because she had to face her unsound behaviour. God made her deal with her faulty conclusions otherwise her follow-up shot would be rendered useless. Warriors need to become different leaders, and as we move into the final stage of our journey in reigniting the warrior within, we shall learn how deal with our personal lives, so we keep on rising well. Don't get discouraged, dear warrior, for when all seems lost this is where the song of the firebird will assist you in your rising. Believe me, the song you'll be singing when your soul is finally free will be something true and beautiful.

Prayer

Dear God,

Help me in the uncomfortable moments of my rising. Teach me what it means to be bold and courageous in voicing my values and beliefs, the ones that I have allowed to be silenced by the crowd. Let me glean from the leadership lessons of Aaron, Miriam, and Moses and how You shaped them as leaders. Please come alongside and help this firebird to grow so I am able to rise to the next level in my leadership. Reveal how my follow-up shot needs to gain some backbone as I slowly let You, God, into my most painful parts of my past so You can work on my fears and insecurities, teaching me to rise up into the responsibility You have entrusted me with. Teach me how to spot the intimidation tactics of the enemy and where he is always trying to make me quit. I choose to stop hiding and stay small, for this isn't what warriors do. I know that if I keep singing the blues it will do me no good, so I want to follow Your instructions and guidance, God because I want my follow-up shot to be made well and to become effective in silencing the enemy. Show me how to sing a different tune and help me to see how much You're cheering me on because You chose me to be Your warrior and You never make mistakes. Let this firebird keep being reminded that believing in myself as much as You believe in me is sometimes the only weapon I'll need.

Amen.

Endnotes: Chapter Seventeen

Ref 1   Miller, Donald. 2003. *Blue Like Jazz: Nonreligious thoughts on Christian Spirituality.* Nahville.Thomas Nelson.

Ref 2   1 Peter 1:4-7 The Passion Translation (the New Testament with Psalms, proverbs, and song of songs.

Ref 3   Knirnschild, Jacqueline.'What's the difference between melody and harmony?' 1st June 2022. Website: nightisalive.com

Ref 4   Bevere, John. 1995. *Breaking Intimidation: How to overcome fear and release the gifts of God in your life.* Charisma House Publishing.

Ref 5   Isaiah 59:16-21: Ecclesia Bible Society. 2012. *The Voice Bible: Step into the Story of Scripture.* Nashville: Thomas Nelson.

Ref 6   Knirnschild, Jacqueline.'What's the difference between melody and harmony?' 1st June 2022. Website: nightisalive.com

Ref 7   Emily P. Freeman. *Grace for the good girl: Letting go of the try hard life.* Revell Publishing 2011.

Ref 8   Exodus 17:8-9: Ecclesia Bible Society. 2012. *The Voice Bible: Step into the Story of Scripture.* Nashville: Thomas Nelson.

Ref 9   Exodus 17:9-15: Ecclesia Bible Society. 2012. *The Voice Bible: Step into the Story of Scripture.* Nashville: Thomas Nelson.

Ref 10   Walton, John H, Victor Harold Matthews, and Mark William Chavalas. 2000.*The IVP Bible Background Commentary Old Testament.* Downers Grove, III. Intervarsity Press.

Ref 11   Website: Crosswalk.com

Ref 12   Website: Biblelyfe.com "Names of God'

Ref 13   Numbers 12:1-5: Ecclesia Bible Society. 2012. *The Voice Bible: Step into the Story of Scripture.* Nashville: Thomas Nelson.

Ref 14   Lencioni, Patrick. 2020. *The Motive: A leadership fable. Why so many leaders abdicate their most important responsibilities.* John Wiley & Sons, New Jersey.

Ref 15   Numbers 12:9-15: Ecclesia Bible Society. 2012. *The Voice Bible: Step into the Story of Scripture.* Nashville, Thomas Nelson.

Ref 16   Wikipedia.org 'Leprosy'

Ref 17   Britannica.com 'Leprosy'

Ref 18   Chand, Samuel R. 2015. *Leadership Pain: The Classroom for Growth.* Nashville, Tennessee, Thomas Nelson.

Ref 19   Numbers 12:15: Ecclesia Bible Society. 2012. *The Voice Bible: Step into the Story of Scripture.* Nashville, Thomas Nelson.

Ref 20   Maxwell, John C. 2018. *Developing the leader within you.* Nashville, Tennessee Nelson Books.

PART FOUR

RISING

CHAPTER EIGHTEEN

Water Song

'And more so, I now realise that all I gained, and thought was important was nothing but yesterday's garbage compared to knowing the Anointed Jesus my Lord.' [1]
PHILIPPIANS 3:8

If you've been speed-reading through this book until now then may I suggest slowing down your pace a little, dear warrior. I understand the story of the Phoenix rising from its own ashes is as inspiring as it is empowering, helping us all to reignite the warrior within. However, if Miriam has taught us anything from the last chapter about her leadership leprosy moment, it's how we respond when we reach the dizzying heights of influence that our song could possibly bring. Stepping up into your warrior role is a marked moment in your story as far as the enemy is concerned. For this reason, as we go through each stage of our transformation and rise up triumphantly out of the flames of affliction, we need to be careful that we don't start coating our feathers in a waterproof sealant that stops the Living Water from penetrating our thirsty souls. The warrior regalia can indeed raise our status and influence in certain circles, and we could possibly find ourselves soaring with eagles because we've finally gained enough courage to leave the chicken coup behind. However, like Miriam, our leadership elevation can reach a point where we become thirsty for more power rather than continuing to draw deeply from the Source that sustains us. Instead of finding the clean, safe water that is found within the well, we become satisfied with surface level water that hasn't been filtered by the soil of God's Word and this unclean water can contaminate our thinking. Clearly Miriam was a strong character as she had a profound effect on the other women in the camp, and if we look back on Miriam's famous tambourine celebration, it affirms just how much influence she had over the other women. But as Vickie Kraft suggests in Miriam's moment of complaint, 'instead of being thankful for the influence God had given her, she wanted more power, more authority, and sometimes when that happens, we lose our influence.'[2] The seven days Miriam was shut out of the camp because of her thirst for power isolated her from the very people she had influenced. Now her confined segregation was influencing others in a different way. If there is one thing you need to remember when you've read the final page of this book and put it back on your bookshelf, it's this. Please, do not allow the enemy a foothold on your influence otherwise he'll steal it, twist it, and use it against you. The magnetic pull of your song that drew people to yourself in the first place ends up attracting the wrong kind of attention if you neglect to steward your influence and power well. Lisa Cron talks about backstories and the power they have by stating, 'the story you're telling doesn't start on page one. It started long before you got there'³ and the *before* in our stories can be used as leverage by the enemy, twisting our influence so that it sends us spiralling back down into the ashes far quicker than the long process it took for us to rise up. When we start losing the *why* in our rising and start obsessing over making ourselves look good then we may as well turn the follow-up shot on ourselves and be done with it.

Okay, that was a little dramatic.

Alright then, let me put it this way. Imagine the enemy has a big highlighter pen and while he's speed-reading your backstory he's highlighting and marking all the points you chose to drink from the easy, surface level water that contaminated your thinking instead of taking the time and effort to find a container to draw clean water found in the deep well of abiding with God. What I mean is, warriors can't live on a diet of a few scraps of scripture verses, little bits of God's Word here and there, it just isn't going to nourish your soul. The enemy scans churches for malnourished warriors who thought they could sustain their calling on a wing and a prayer. And as the devil circles overhead like a vulture getting ready to pick at the bones of your backstory, he's hoping to highlight all *that stuff* you thought was dead and buried. Make no mistake, you wouldn't be the first person whose influence was turned against them by the enemy, and sadly, if you don't steward your warrior calling well, then you certainly won't be the last.

Power Play

With all this talk of rising, David asks in Psalm 24, 'Who can climb Mount God? Who can scale the holy north-face? Only the clean-handed, only pure-hearted; men who won't cheat, women who won't seduce. God is at their side; with God's help they make it.'[4] Clean hands and a pure heart washed by the Living Water Himself cures our appetites for more power and prestige. It launders all the dust and grime in our 'desire of wanting to get a following to be well known, to get a reputation'[5] so we don't seek to gain more power. When we choose to lower our containers deep into God's well, it scoops up all the things we've tried to bury, bringing them up to the surface so God can deal with our sin. Miriam's backstory found her with no influence or power and her rising up the ranks to prophetess and amazing worship leader would have possibly been a heady experience. Considering her life theme is water, she forgot to draw deeply from the well of the never-ending supply of fresh revelation from God when she told Moses what she thought of her new, foreign sister-in-law and why God should only speak to Moses on an intimate level. A rich, satisfying, abundant flow of water would have cleaned up every contaminated thought of, 'I wish I could do *that*' or, 'I wish I was like *her* or *him*.' Miriam's isolation revealed what was really going on inside of her, and if that wildfire burning within her was left unattended, God knew it would eventually consume Miriam completely. Sometimes the most dangerous fires we go through in our rising are the ones that can destroy us from within, and a lust for power means we haven't dug deep enough down into the life-giving well of Living Water that satisfies our every need for recognition, power, and acknowledgement.

A Stunning Anthem

I'm not suggesting that unless you have it altogether God is never going to bestow warriorship upon you. There is no backstory, regardless of how many coloured highlighter pens the enemy has used to point out your flaws, that God cannot deliver and redeem you from. He's not waiting with His sword poised hoping you'll come up through the flames of your past so squeaky clean that He'll need dark glasses to look at you as He's saying the words, 'Warrior, you may now rise' because if you're thinking that, then you are going to have to start digging into the Scriptures and read about the biblical heroes God used for His glory. The ones that had no status or pedigree, the people who were looked over and looked down upon, those were the ones whom God chose and anointed for greatness. Every one of them a flawed, sinful human who stumbled and fell multiple times until they tapped into the Living Water source found in God that sustained their calling. It's our motives and agendas that need to be washed over and over in the well so the warrior trait of helping others shines through. As Paul says in Romans chapter 15, 'Strength is for service, not status. Each one of us needs to look after the good of the people around us, asking ourselves, "How can I help?"' God wants the combination of His steady, constant calling and warm, personal counsel in Scripture to characterise us, keeping us alert for whatever He will do next. May our dependably steady and warmly personal God develop maturity in you so that you get along with each other as well as Jesus gets along with us all. Then we'll be a choir—not our voices only, but our very lives singing in harmony in a stunning anthem to the God and Father of our Master Jesus!'[6] Read that passage again and allow it to sink into your soul for a second. Warriors who *know* that their strength is for service and not for status never drink from the contaminated shallow waters of prestige and power because their very lives, not just their voices sing a stunning anthem. Take a tip from me, don't look at others and start drawing conclusions on who God should and shouldn't use as His warriors, else we'll be playing the power game that nobody wins. God isn't too worried about your backstory, He's far more concerned when His people start going all Egyptian on Him as we try to mummify our past, so it preserves our reputations.

Flick open your Bible and draw from the story of the Samaritan women found in John chapter 4 as she asks Jesus where the living water He's offering comes from and you'll soon discover Jesus is more interested in someone coming clean about needing Him than how many husbands they've had. The devil is obsessed with sifting through the debris of your backstory, trying to find one grain of evidence he can use to turn your influence against you. You'll notice after reading the story of the woman at the well, she left her water jar behind because she felt she didn't need it anymore. When this woman first met Jesus, she was drawing conclusions and had her water jar ready, however, by the end of the conversation with the Living Water, she realised she'd tapped into a never-ending water supply that satisfied every part of her parched soul. The One who helped heal her shame and fulfill her deepest longings because she decided to be honest with Him and come clean. 'Many of the Samaritans from that village committed themselves to Him because of the woman's witness: "He knew all about the things I did. He knows me inside and out!" They asked him to stay on, so Jesus stayed two days.' [7] Trust me, dear warrior, God knows us from the inside out and He still chooses us anyway. When we become completely satisfied and content because we're deciding to continually draw from the Living Water, this is where deep calls to deep in our song.

'In the roar of Your waterfalls,
ancient depths surge,
calling out to the deep.
All Your waves break over me; am I drowning?
Yet in the light of day,
the Eternal shows me His love.
When night settles in and all is dark,
He keeps me company—
His soothing song, a prayerful melody
to the True God of my life.'[8]

Endnotes: Chapter Eighteen

Ref 1   Philippians 3:8: Ecclesia Bible Society. 2012. *The Voice Bible: Step into the Story of Scripture.* Nashville: Thomas Nelson.

Ref 2   Kraft, Vickie. Bible.org Women of the Bible. 'Lesson 1: Miriam.'

Ref 3   Cron, Lisa. 2016. *Story Genius: How to use brain science to go beyond outlining and write a riveting novel (before You Waste Three Years Writing 327 Pages That Go Nowhere).* Berkeley: Ten Speed Press.

Ref 4   Psalm 24:3-4: Colossians 3:12-14: Peterson, Eugene H. 1995. *The Message Bible.* Colorado Springs, Co: Navpress.

Ref 5   Tozer, A.W, and James L. Snyder. 2011. *The Essential Tozer Collection 3-In-1.* Bethany House Publishers.

Ref 6   Romans 15:2-6: Colossians 3:12-14: Peterson, Eugene H. 1995. *The Message Bible.* Colorado Springs, Co: Navpress.

Ref 7   John 4:39-41: Colossians 3:12-14: Peterson, Eugene H. 1995. *The Message Bible.* Colorado Springs, Co: Navpress.

Ref 8   Psalm 43:7-8: Ecclesia Bible Society. 2012. *The Voice Bible: Step into the Story of Scripture.* Nashville: Thomas Nelson.

CHAPTER NINETEEN

Calling Out from the Deep

'A life lived for others, is the only life worth living' [1]
ALBERT EINSTEIN

Characteristically, the Exodus story is about divine rescue. It's the reclaiming, recovering, and restoring of God's people, and this story of the Israelites deliverance from slavery to freedom gains its momentum in the telling and retelling over the generations. This is why Miriam's memoir has been so necessary in helping you to reconnect and reignite the warrior within as she recounts and runs through each step of her story in her own rising, helping boost your confidence to rise up from the ashes of all your yesterdays and into the freedom found in each one of your tomorrows. The narrative of your follow-up shot can disperse shrapnel like a confetti canon into the enemy's camp each time you tell and retell what the Lord has delivered you from, and it is this part in your song that the enemy will want to dissuade and hinder in your rising. If anything, Miriam's life has taught us how to sing a song that has words and a melody that our wounding caused us to forget for a little while, and the retelling of her story has encouraged us to raise our weapons of warfare as we stand on the promises of God. Glen O'Brien highlights the fact that our worship has a narrative element to it, and as we come together as believers, singing our songs of deliverance, we retell the story of Christ's life, death, and resurrection.[2] He goes on to say that 'the origin of the English word "worship" is the old English "worth ship", meaning to attribute worth to a person or thing.'[2] Acknowledging what God has done for us, narrating over and over again the story that He is worthy to receive all our praise and worship are the components found within the inner parts of a firebird's song that the devil is most concerned about. Because regardless of his tactics and schemes in making sure we were kept silent, we've managed to find our voices that now echo and reverberate what God has delivered us from, and it's a song we're unlikely to forget. This calling out from the deep, this intimacy, this renewed dedication to God in our worship, this is what gets our enemy into a tizzy. Now that the warrior within us has been ignited we can keep telling and retelling our stories of what God has brought us through, giving the devil's plan of attack no legs to stand on, causing that slippery snake of old to give up, give back, and relinquish the ground he has stolen from us because our song rising reminds the devil that we are no longer running, for the turning of the tide has come and now *he's* the one running. As true worshippers we become intimate with Jesus in a way we didn't experience before, for in our running the flames were being fanned by our guilt and shame. However, now the fire within is being fuelled by our awe and wonder of God's divine rescue that has brought us out from the slavery of our past into the freedom Jesus died for.

Told and Retold

Storytelling was an important aspect of Old Testament life as the stories which were told and retold helped to solidify the Israelites beliefs and values from one generation to the next. In my own family, and I'm sure in yours too, information shared over the years has kept reenforcing the ideology within our families as stories get passed down from one generation to the other. The layers of history found in the stories of the Bible, ancient accounts that help us to join in the 'ongoing conversation that goes back at least 2,500 years'[3] that shares its truth that God is the Redeemer and Deliverer of His people. The One who 'bestows on them a crown of beauty instead of ashes, the oil of gladness instead of mourning, and a garment of praise instead of a spirit of despair.'[4] A love story that is constantly getting told and retold every time we read about the One who will never abandon His wounded ones and helps them to soar into their futures. Your song is rising, dear warrior, and when we dig deep into the Scriptures we are reminded over and over how God keeps His promises.

Miriam has been our mentor along this long journey in reigniting the warrior within, and she has taught us how to use our weapon of song well against the enemy's schemes, and our follow-up shot will indeed serve us well. This great prophetess and worship leader has shared her story with truth and vulnerability, showing us each one of the well-worn, ancient stepping stones that guide us into the way of the warrior. A path that has no alternate, easier route to our purpose as we rise up from the ashes. The lessons we have learned from Miriam's life we shall never stop gleaning from and the little cabin in the forest we were so afraid to leave before our journey began, now becomes a monument, a testimony that God has more for you, dear warrior, than just the healing of your wounds. No more looking back, He wants His warriors to be as strategic as they are savvy because your song that is rising will help others find their way too as your story encourages them to move out from the dust and dirt of their past mistakes and into a brighter future.

Out of Tune

Imagine if we had only focused on the good parts of Miriam's story and left out all the bad parts? Would her story have the same depth? Would it be loud enough and clear enough to echo her truth through the corridors of time? I highly doubt it. There is a danger we can leave out some of the not-so-great details in our story to make the notes in our song sound more like a great symphony than something that resembles a cat's chorus. Specific memories that have left their marks on your precious, scarred heart that you'd rather not share, if you don't mind. I have to admit, while writing my testimony in *Wounded And On The Run*, it felt like I was dousing myself with paraffin and then striking a match as it got nearer and nearer to its release date. My carefully crafted image and people's perceived perceptions of me were about to get blown sky high after they'd read the truth within my story, and I realised that the stigma of my past may find me neck deep back in the ash pile I'd be trying to dig my way out of for what felt like—*forever*. It's like the enemy hissed into my ear, 'After this little bomb shell, they'll be no rising for you, pathetic, little firebird. When people hear your truth, you'll never get out of those ashes alive.'

All those incidents and accidents I'd experienced decades ago could mean that everyone wouldn't hear my song rising, only the rattling of bones from all the skeletons in the cupboard I'd so desperately tried to keep silent. However, I knew if I wanted to help others to walk into the freedom Jesus died for, I needed to tell my story, warts, and all. And although it wasn't pitch perfect, it was my story, my truth, and my song. That's the thing about our stories, we've spent so long running away from that monster that sits waiting underneath our beds, so many years trying to hide all the details of what makes up the parts of our song, that we end up making up a fictious fable that sounds far better than the truth. To be honest, I sobbed as I wrote some of the chapters in my first book, and it wasn't because my wounds hadn't turned into scars, it was because I was in a mud wrestle with shame that had attached itself to each note of my song that I was struggling with. The thing is, God didn't want me to fabricate the details of my story, so it sounded pitch perfect. He never asked me to polish up my song before He could use it to help others who were being blood trailed by the hunter, Satan. He didn't want my song to impress to the point where people felt too unqualified, too flawed, too damaged, and too wounded to connect their story with mine. God needed me to become the guide, who would lead others truthfully back to His heart. Now a year on since the release of my book, I have lost count the number of testimonies from my readers who can identify with my story, and how my song helped them to discover the healing power found in the scars on the hands and feet of Jesus to heal their wounds too. What if I had left out all the not-so-great parts of my song? Would it have had the same impact on others if I'd just shared all the good notes? Possibly not. When we sing our song with honesty our story connects with others and it becomes a powerful weapon against the enemy's lies. When the narrative of our stories sound more myth than memoir, then we've forgotten the power of why we tell and retell them. As Donald Miller highlights a palliative care nurse's response when asked about regrets, she said that her patients who have only a few weeks left to live, 'wished they'd had the courage to live a life true to themselves and not the life others expected of them.'[5] I don't know about you, dear warrior, but I don't want to live a life out of tune with the truth of who I am, of who God called me to be. The only way we're going to counteract the lies of the enemy is for others to hear the truth of our song. Because that, dear firebird, is where you'll spread your wings and rise up with confidence into the fresh air of your freedom.

Endnotes: Chapter Nineteen

Ref 1   Kirby, Stephanie. 2023. everydaypower.com/pay-it-forward-quotes/ 'Pay it forward Quotes to help you live a better life' Updated May 10.

Ref 2   O'Brien, Glen. 2013. *Christian Worship. A Theological and Historical Introduction* Morning Star Publishing. (Borrowed From University of Wollongong Library)

Ref 3   Hubbard, Robert L. Jr, and J. Andrew Dearman. 2018. *Introducing the Old Testament.* Grand Rapids.

Ref 4   Isaiah 61:3: Syswerda, Jean, and Faith Organization.2001. NIV Women of Faith Study Bible: New International Version. Grand Rapids, Mich.: Zondervan.

Ref 5   Miller, Donald. 2015. *Scary Close: Dropping the Act and Finding True Intimacy.* Nashville, Tennessee. Thomas Nelson.

CHAPTER TWENTY

Home Will Be Found

'There comes a special moment in everyone's life, a moment for which that person was born. That special opportunity, when he seizes it, will fulfill his mission—a mission for which he is uniquely qualified. In that moment, he will find greatness. It is his finest hour.'[1]
WINSTON CHURCHILL

I know you've been wanting to ask a question that's possibly been bugging you for quite a few chapters. You're wondering when does the Phoenix actually set fire to itself? We're now right in the thick of the book of Numbers and as we follow our guide, Miriam, under the shade of the green, living canopy high above our heads that is made up from the large branches of the trees either side of the stony path, we're moving toward the sound of a waterfall. You glance at Miriam as we get closer and closer to the noise of the rushing water and note that her steps seem to be slowing down as her dusty sandals shuffle along the stony path. You think back to the moment you first met our brave warrior guide outside the little wooden cabin in the forest, remembering all your preconceived ideas and perceptions of how this leader could actually help you to rise up from the ashes of your past and reignite the warrior within. Things have certainly changed as you gotten to know Miriam better, and as this journey has unfolded, you've found yourself observing and admiring this legendary woman more and more. The mature woman beside you, whose story has been shared so authentically, of how she became a sister, a prophetess, and worship warrior in the ancient text throughout the Exodus story, has made you acutely aware of how each well-weathered line on her radiant, ageing face are the marks of a true warrior who has learned how to trust God fully regardless of each circumstance she found herself in. It seems Miriam is becoming more frail the nearer we get to the waterfall. You wonder if perhaps all this trekking over high mountains and into the deep valleys and caves has possibly taken its toll on her? You have to admit, a hot meal and a cosy bed would be a welcome relief after spending many hours out in the harsh wilderness. Miriam quietly walks beside you while you're pondering on this warrior journey. It's like you're together, step-by-step, in sync with one another, and then she turns to you and says, 'You want to know when the Phoenix sets fire to itself. Well, after living for 500 years, the Phoenix builds a nest just before its time is up. That is the moment it sets fire to itself.'[2] Oh my, it's like she's read your mind. You answer her with a silent nod. This is something to quietly consider rather than to respond with a multitude of words. When we finally reach the waterfall, Miriam gestures to a bench and comments on resting for a moment so she can catch her breath. Miriam's answer about the Phoenix rolls around in your mind as we sit quietly while we listen to the rushing water splash down onto the rocks. Finally, you speak. 'Why is it *that* moment when the Phoenix feels it's becoming weak and old that it then sets fire to itself?' Miriam closes her eyes and listens to the rushing water for a few moments before she responds. 'It is this season of weakness when the Phoenix believes it's too tired and too old that it undergoes its full resurrection and rebirth' she finally answers. In some way you understand that this warrior woman has fulfilled her assignment in helping you to reignite the warrior within. Somehow you know that it's time to say goodbye to this audacious leader.

We've followed Miriam right throughout the Exodus story, and sadly, it is indeed time for this brave woman to leave us. 'After the Israelites, the whole group of them journeyed into the Zin Wilderness during the first month, they set up camp in Kadesh. And it was there that Miriam died and was buried. They ran out of water and again blamed their leaders, Moses, and Aaron.'[3]

Wait!

That's it?

This significant warrior's life has been all wrapped up in a death sentence that consists of only five words! You close your eyes and think about each word. Miriam... died... and... was... buried. Seems a little underrated, a little brief to not give the older sister of the greatest Bible hero of all time a much more considerable amount of recognition than this sparse eulogy. Feels a tad insulting that she only gets five words to describe her death. After this wrestle with your emotions and petitions in your mind, you open your eyes and discover Miriam has slipped away unnoticed. Your attention is drawn to a gold plaque that is screwed into one of the wooden slats on the bench and you read aloud the inscription.

'The peace warrior knows the way
Her counsel gathers round her
And fixes to smother her burn,
Only to encourage new light
To emit.
Squeezing out the rays
The ways of the
Peaceful warrior,
To be spread along with the wind
And the breath of God.
I welcome all that is within.
I set myself on fire!
Focused on the light

I choose this path
The steps are clearer now'[4]

How fitting. A memorial bench to commemorate the heroic life of Miriam. A brave woman who became a prophetess, a worship leader, and a warrior whose story of song will go on to inspire many generations and help them to leave behind the ashes of their past, reigniting the warrior within, helping them to rise in the knowledge that God will *never* abandon them.

The Ashes of Sacrifice

If we just pause in our reflection of Miriam's life for a moment and back track to chapter nineteen in the book of Numbers, we'll find that before Miriam's death God is reminding Moses and Aaron about purity rituals.

Let's look at Numbers 19:2-10, shall we? 'I want to remind you about a decree of instruction by my command: "When they need to make a sin offering, instruct the Israelites to bring a young female cow, red in colour, that is perfect in every visible way and has never worked. Hand it over to the priest, Eleazar. He will then oversee it slaughter outside the camp, dip his finger in the blood, splatter the blood seven times in the direction of the congregation tent's opening, and make sure that the carcass is burned, every bit if it—hide, flesh, blood, and dung. While the cow burns, the priest will throw onto the fire some aromatic woods—cedar and hyssop—bound together by scarlet thread. Afterward, the priest should carefully wash himself and his clothes; then he can re-enter the camp. Likewise, the one who burns the fire should also wash himself and his clothes. But recognize that they are ritually impure until that evening. Someone else, someone ritually pure, should collect the ashes that remain from the completely burnt offering and put them all in a ritually pure place outside the boundaries of the camp. Then that person, too, should wash his clothes and understand he is ritually impure until evening. The ashes will be used to make a cleansing solution for the Israelites. This is a sin offering.'[5] It's worth noting that this instruction from God is placed right before Miriam's death. The fact that the heifer had to be red in colour, needed to be female, slaughtered, not sacrificed, killed outside camp and not at the altar, and then burned whole are specific instructions from the Eternal One that represent a distinct offering.[6] This ancient Near East cleansing ritual was because a person who had been contaminated by a corpse, made them ceremonially unclean. The mixture of ashes from the sacrificial red heifer and water coming from a running stream was known as water cleansing.[7] It is suggested that the significance of the ashes and water theme represents 'the ashes of Christ's merit, and the water of His Spirit' meaning the work of Christ, together with the Spirit of God through his Word, brought cleansing from the impurities surrounding death.[8] Also, it is interesting to note, that 'the unclean person had to be sprinkled with the specific water from the water cleansing ritual on the third and seventh day. The numbers three and seven signify fullness or completion.'[9] I may be taking a stab in the dark with my thinking, but I see the parallels of the Phoenix's story. The red coloured plumage of the firebird resembles the red heifer. The ashes from our past and the water theme of Miriam's life feels similar to our warrior journey. Curiously after Miriam's death, the well dried up leaving the camp's survival in dire straits. Perhaps this was something to do with Miriam's water theme? Who knows. However, we do know the Israelites started blaming their leaders, Moses, and Aaron for the lack of water.

Miriam had played her part in the Exodus story and was now at rest. She had found her eternal home and she would be greatly missed. The warrior who had taken her tambourine and led the women in a worship song. The brave one who had trusted and relied upon God for His protection and provision was now gone and her absence had caused the water to dry up. Wondering if God was going to abandon them and leave them to die in the desert, the Israelites complained to Moses and Aaron. Would they ever learn from their past mistakes and realise their misguided view about God's lack of care and provision was always going to end up with them facing some severe consequences.

Homeward Bound

Forty long, hard years in the wilderness. Miriam had died, the Israelites were complaining there was no water. Could it get any worse? Oh, yes it can. Moses and Aaron decided to intercede for the people and God gives them some instructions. "You and Aaron grab the staff before the covenant chest, gather the whole group so that all the people can see and hear you, and speak to the rock. Tell it to release its water for them to use. In this way, you'll get water from the rock for everyone to drink, including all the animals." So, Moses did that. He took the staff just as God told him to do. Then he and his brother gathered all the people in front of the rock. "Listen up, you rebellious lot. Should we get water for you from this rock?" As he spoke, Moses raised his hand and hit the rock—once, twice—and immediately the water came gushing out. All drank their fill, people, and animals alike. But the Eternal One scolded Moses and Aaron for their actions. "Because you didn't trust Me and treat Me as holy before the Israelites, you will not lead this group into the land I have given them."' [10] And just like that, Moses' dream of living out the rest of his days in the Promised Land lands him knee deep in the ash pile. Brace yourself, there's more. God instructs Moses to take his brother up to Mount Hor and strip him of his priestly robes and put them on Aaron's son, Eleazar.

The text says, 'And Aaron died there.'[11] Unlike his big sister, the High Priest, Aaron, gets only four words in his obituary. What about Moses? Well, he doesn't enter his eternal home until Deuteronomy chapter 34, and just to note; his obituary gets a whole three verses. Three warriors gone and the gift they left behind was the gift of a song that had been crafted for forty years. Their story became the follow-up shot for the next generation to listen out for and use the notes to advance God's kingdom. Miriam, Aaron, and Moses' feet may have become hard and calloused from walking the desert plains. Their faces may have been weathered and lined by the harsh conditions of the wilderness; however, their warrior spirits helped them to rise up from their circumstances and fully trust God for their provision, and for that, they are to be honoured and appreciated. Especially Miriam, our fearless leader whose careful hand has guided us right throughout our warrior journey. The tambourine waving warrior who knew who she was and more importantly, *Whose* she was. Listen carefully, her song is still being heard through the corridors of time, the one resounding loud and clear and is aimed straight into enemy territory. Reminding him that our God, the Eternal One, Yahweh, is to be worshipped, trusted, and adored.

The Biggest Lie

Encouraging the next generation to rise up is a great thing to do and I'm all for cheering them on, however, some of you warriors reading this book may feel like you're a little too ancient of days to believe you have something to offer. You're considering laying down your warrior sword and hanging up your battle-worn armour, allowing some elbow room for the younger generation to start claiming back the territory the enemy has taken. You'll admit that you're weary, and besides, your throat feels hoarse from singing your song, so perhaps it's time to pass the baton and let the younger ones fight on the battlefield. Remember what Miriam said? 'It is this season of weakness, of believing you're too tired that the metaphor of the Phoenix undergoes its resurrection and rebirth.' The enemy wants you think that you've done your service and now it's time to hang up your warrior boots and retire. He's happy to fan the flames in your thinking that your voice has lost its authority and the sound of your song is going to be ignored by the next generation. Interestingly, one of the synonyms for aged is 'shot' and I'm here to remind you that we need your follow-up shot song.

It matters. You matter.

For the enemy is aiming to 'take out the generals and high-ranking officers' in the overcomers army by silencing your voice.[12] As Jill Austin says, 'The biggest lie (we) hear from the enemy is that (we are) beyond the point of having something to give.'[12] She adds, '(we've) become spectators in the grandstands.' Being a warrior is not about becoming a spectator, there's no time for bystanders when there is ground to be reclaimed. Many are laying in the ashes of their past just waiting for a firebird to help raise them up and point them to Jesus.

This is your finest hour.

This is your resurrection and rebirth.

So, clear your throat, dear warrior, and let your song be heard!

Endnotes: Chapter Twenty

Ref 1   azquotes.com

Ref 2   Sundstrom, Bob. 2023. 'The Legendary Phoenix' Website: birdnote.org. April 22,

Ref 3   Numbers 20:1-2: Ecclesia Bible Society. 2012. *The Voice Bible: Step into the Story of Scripture.* Nashville: Thomas Nelson.

Ref 4   Seven, Seher. 2015. 'Warrior' Poem. Website: hellopoetry.com

Ref 5   Numbers 19:2-10: Ecclesia Bible Society. 2012. *The Voice Bible: Step into the Story of Scripture.* Nashville: Thomas Nelson.

Ref 6   Guzik, David. 2023. Enduring word Bible commentary on Numbers 19. Website: enduringword.com

Ref 7   Walton, John H, Victor Harold Matthews, and Mark William Chavalas. 2000.*The IVP Bible Background Commentary Old Testament.* Downers Grove, Ill. Intervarsity Press.

Ref 8   Guzik, David. 2023. Enduring word Bible commentary on Numbers 19. Website: enduringword.com

Ref 9   Biblical commentary on Numbers 19: Syswerda, Jean, and Faith Organization.2001. NIV Women of Faith Study Bible: New International Version. Grand Rapids, Mich.: Zondervan.

Ref 10   Numbers 20:6-12: Ecclesia Bible Society. 2012. *The Voice Bible: Step into the Story of Scripture.* Nashville: Thomas Nelson.

Ref 11   Numbers 20:27-28: Ecclesia Bible Society. 2012. *The Voice Bible: Step into the Story of Scripture.* Nashville: Thomas Nelson.

Ref 12   Austin, Jill. 2007. *Dancing with destiny : Awaken your heart to dream, to love, to war.*   Grand Rapids. Chosen Books Publishing.

CHAPTER TWENTY-ONE

A Song is Rising

'I am proof that one person can rise above any challenge, and if I can, then so will others if they are given the chance.'[1]
EMMANUEL JAL

A fifth-century, Christian theologian by the name of St Peter Chrysologus, is thought to have written about a bird that would rise up from the ashes and glorify God by singing praises to Him. Also, the Phoenix story is known to symbolise the Exodus story, paralleling the Israelites leaving the slavery of Egypt and rising up into the freedom of the Promised Land.[2] I see these as footprints along the warrior path that have been left behind for us to follow so we are able to find the courage to rise up and sing our song. I do hope that this journey you've bravely embarked on in reigniting the warrior within, has not only taught you that you'll never be abandoned by God, but the Phoenix rising up from its own ashes has shown you that there are better things to come. Some parts of this journey have possibly left you feeling as though you've been through a cremation rather than a celebration. However, there's no resurrection unless there has been a death first, right? And Miriam's life can testify that 'nobody appreciates deliverance like those who've nearly been destroyed.'³ God is always encouraging us to keep moving forward and to keep looking ahead rather than looking behind us, for it is in the remembering of our stories, not the setting up camp in them that helps others to rise. Our past has shaped and formed us into who we are today, and God is using each wounded warrior because of our painful pasts, not in spite of it. A song is rising from the ones who have known the pain of heartbreak and wounding, but it is through the ashes of grief that we have learned how to rise once again. Now is not the time to stand still, dear warrior, because there are many more who need to hear your follow-up shot that will help them rise up from the ashes of their past too. Warriors are on the move and the melody we are singing, the beat sheet we're marching to, lets the enemy know that the God of the Angel Armies is on our side because He has given us beauty from ashes and has awakened a chorus of overcomers who have learned how to rise, take flight, and reignite the warrior within.

Stay with Him

Now that you've reignited the warrior within, the enemy will try his best to silence your song with his intimidation tactics. The strongman will come and try to steal your inheritance, the birthright that was fought for at the cross, however, you now know better, dear warrior, for it will be the devil who will be intimidated by your rising and he'll be the one running when he hears your follow-up shot coming. There's no lie you can't uncover, the one that tries to hoodwink you, telling you that God will indeed abandon you, for that myth isn't going to fly now. As the prophet Jerimiah says, 'But I am not alone. The Eternal is here with me. He stands beside me, as a dreaded warrior. That is why my tormentors will fail so miserably. They cannot win.'[4] The refiner's fire has burned up any dross in your thinking that you'll be taken so far with God and then left to fend for yourself. Be selective in listening to thoughts that come into your mind and take no notice of the ones that keep telling you that you're not good enough, not worthy enough, not capable enough to be held and cared for by God. Sift through them until you get to the truth of the matter, knowing that you are cherished, loved, and valued by the One who parted the waves for your rescue, bringing you up out of a place that had shackled your wings, setting you free from the chains designed to stop you from rising. Harry A. Overstreet points out that, 'The immature mind hops from one thing to another; the mature mind seeks to follow through.'[5] Warriors always follow through and Miriam's leading throughout this journey, although difficult at times, has matured you into a warrior who will finish what they started. A fighter whose song has been shaped and sharpened into a weapon that will silence the enemy into the shadows of retreat. Through the retelling of Miriam's story, our tambourine waving, worship warrior has taught us that by trusting God completely we are able to rise up from the ashes of our past and become the warrior we were meant to be. As the saying goes, 'Birds of a feather flock together' and we are joined together, with the saints who have marched to the beat of their song before us and to the wounded ones behind us who are yet to hear our song. Warriors standing together, side by side, arm in arm, the ones who have each other's backs and who sing the song of what God has delivered them through. Play your follow-up shot on repeat so you never forget everything God brought you through and delivered you from. Just know, dear warrior, that your flight is not going to be all plain sailing from now on. The enemy is onto you, and he will use the same schemes that caused you to run in the first place. But, as our fearless leader, Miriam has taught us, 'it is the (ones) who remembered to grab their tambourines'[6] that will lead others into worshipping Yahweh. The God who rescued His people when a Pharaoh was chasing behind them and the waters were too deep in front of them. Their God, who is *still* our God, the One who never changes, who is worthy of our tambourine song, the Eternal who turned impossible into possible and made a way when there wasn't one. We, the wounded ones, now know better than to listen to the sound coming from the enemy's camp because God ain't raising no fools, for the water theme of Miriam's life reminds the wounded warriors to...

Stay with Him.

When you have to tell a different story to the one Pharaoh dictates to you.

Stay with Him.

When you need to approach powerful people, like Pharaoh's daughter, so your family is saved.

Stay with Him.

When you're only seeing impossible behind and in front of you and all you've packed is a tambourine.

Stay with Him.

When your focus is distracted by Golden Calves and someone else's wardrobe.

Stay with Him.

When you've been disciplined by God because you fell into the trap of wanting more influence and power in your leadership role.

Stay with Him.

When you're feeling too old and weary to rise up from the ashes.

Stay with Him.

Stay with Him.

Stay with Him.

This is the peace warrior's carry when they've allowed God to set their faith on fire. Follow Him with your follow-up shot that is locked and loaded with your song, dear warrior, and watch the enemy get silenced into submission.

Look for the Signposts

The trajectory of your journey has helped you to become airborne, dear firebird, and no doubt, there will be updrafts and downdrafts as you continue in the direction of the sacred way of the warrior. This journey was about resilience, strength and determination, a song that rises from our lips and is sung because it is our life song. You've learned along the way to trust God even when the pain has been deep and you didn't think you'd take another step. Even in the midst of your struggles and doubts you've found your way through the ashes and pushed through the discomfort so you're able to rise into the future God has for you. The enemy may try to hinder your flight path, but the more you embrace the truth that God will never abandon you then the more you'll learn to trust God regardless of your circumstances. Not only are our stories of wounding entwining us to each other, so we don't feel alone, but our song has tied us securely to the One who leads us because 'He'll be with you, and He'll never fail you or abandon you. So, don't be afraid.'[7]

If you find yourself shrinking back into the ashes because you're too scared that your song will be heard, then know these are the signposts to look out for that are pointing toward silencing your voice. There is a strength in your surrender that the enemy knows nothing about, for the word *surrender* is a foreign concept to a fallen angel who was kicked out of heaven because of his pride. Wounded ones are tired of hearing songs that have no depth or power, leaving them empty-handed and unequipped because there has been no cost to the follow-up shot. Unless we surrender ourselves fully to God's plan, we could have never risen up from the ashes if we had decided to do it our own way. Many believers, as A.W. Tozer suggests, 'like to have a little glory for (themselves)... willing to let God have most of it, but (wanting) a commission, just a little bit for (themselves)... wanting to rescue part of (themselves) from the cost.' Wannabe warriors are unwilling to pay the price of surrendering to God's plan that will help, not just ourselves, but others to rise. True warriors never direct their precious energy into defending themselves when they've set their faith in the firm foundations of Christ. Reigniting the warrior within makes sure *that lie* doesn't get any airtime in our thinking. The power of our follow-up shot comes from the intimacy we share with the One who has delivered us and showed us His scars that tell His story of how He rescued us from the ashes. The One who saw the personal cost of His song in the agony of the cross and rose again on the third day, reminding us that we were worth every cent of the asking price. Vulnerable, authentic, intimacy keeps us out of the shadows of hiding because shame can no longer narrate the rest of our stories. Your story, your follow-up shot, your song will give others hope that better days are coming, and you'll remind the wounded ones that God always makes a way possible when impossible is all that's in front and behind. Rise up, dear warrior, and use your follow-up shot well. The enemy can see that you're now not afraid of the unknown, the not-quite-yet, or the in-between-a-rock-and-the-hard-places because you've learned to trust God fully and completely in every situation and in every circumstance you find yourself in.

Remember to fly high, dear firebird, and make sure you sing loud...

Prayer

Dear God,

Help me to find the clean, safe water that is found within the well and not become satisfied with surface level water that hasn't been filtered by the soil of Your Word. Show me where a dangerous fire has started that could destroy me from within, revealing to me that I haven't dug deep enough down into the life-giving well of You, the Living Water, that satisfies my every need. I no longer look toward the shallowness of recognition, power, and acknowledgement from others, only Your attention is worth running toward. I renew my dedication to You, God, now that the warrior within me has been ignited I am able to keep telling and retelling my story of what You, God have brought me through. The devil has to relinquish the ground he has stolen from me because my song is rising, reminding him that I am no longer running. I want to become a true worshipper. I want to become intimate with You in a way I've never experienced before. Let the fire within me be fuelled by my awe and wonder of Your divine rescue, bringing me out from the slavery of my past and into the freedom of my future that Jesus died for. I am no longer a spectator because there is ground to be reclaimed, to be taken back from the enemy and I will use my follow-up shot to help claim back that territory. I understand many other wounded ones are laying in the ashes of their past just waiting for a firebird, like me, to help raise them up and point them to Jesus. This is my finest hour. This is my resurrection and rebirth. Thank you, God, for helping me to find my voice and now my song is going to be heard.
Amen.

Now that your warrior journey is over, and Miriam, our faith-filled guide has departed, you're wondering when we'll be heading back to the little wooden cabin in the forest. Somehow, you feel different from when you first embarked on this warrior journey and you're looking forward to using your follow-up shot so others can hear your song. Ah, dear firebird, your journey isn't over yet. It's not time to head back to the safety of the little wooden cabin in the forest, for there is another guide I want you to meet. Someone who tells us in Galatians 6:17 that he 'bears on his body the marks of Jesus.'[9] Yes, the apostle Paul is going to teach God's warriors how to soar higher. Paul is going show us that there is strength in our surrender if we will be daring enough to live the Gethsemane life.

Endnotes: Chapter Twenty-One

Ref 1   brainyquote.com 'Rise Above' Quotes.

Ref 2   Wall, Kimberly. 2022. 'The meaning of Phoenix in the Bible and what it symbolize.' Website: biblekeeper.com

Ref 3   Moore, Beth. 'A Dance In The Desert' Sermon. YouTube watch.

Ref 4   Jerimiah 20:11: Ecclesia Bible Society. 2012. *The Voice Bible: Step into the Story of Scripture.* Nashville: Thomas Nelson.

Ref 5   The Word For Today, Vision Christian Media Devotional. March, 2023.

Ref 6   Voskamp, Ann. 2022. *Waymaker : Finding the Way to the Life You've Always Dreamed Of.* Nahville, Tennessee: W Publishing Group, An Imprint Of Thomas Nelson.

Ref 7   Deuteronomy 31:8: Ecclesia Bible Society. 2012. *The Voice Bible: Step into the Story of Scripture.* Nashville: Thomas Nelson.

Ref 8   Tozer, A.W, and James L. Snyder. 2011. *The Essential Tozer Collection 3-In-1.* Bethany House Publishers.

Ref 9   Galatians 6:17: Ecclesia Bible Society. 2012. *The Voice Bible: Step into the Story of Scripture.* Nashville: Thomas Nelson.

Ref 10   Google question search: Is soaring different to flying?

ONE FINAL THOUGHT...

As I mentioned at the start of our journey, this book is your follow-up shot. A weapon to aim straight at the enemy so his tactics and schemes cannot leave you so easily wounded and on the run. This piece of armoury, dear reawakened warrior, is for you to wield along your journey and has been custom-made and shaped by the song of your testimony that sings about how Yahweh, the One who redeemed and rescued His people out of the slavery of Egypt and into the freedom that was their God-given inheritance of the Promised Land, has rescued and redeemed you too because He loves you so. The melody you sing is a beat sheet that keeps reminding the enemy that through every one of your heartbreaks and each one of your breakthroughs you chose to raise your tambourine and sing of God's goodness and grace regardless of the circumstances you found yourself facing, letting the enemy know that he has undeniably messed with the wrong person because the warrior within has truly been reignited. Tenacity, grit, and abiding in God's unfailing love will see you through the next phase of the journey, dear warrior, regardless of what the enemy tries to undo or distract you with. And yet, you're wondering, what if I cannot soar out of the flames like the Phoenix did? What if I become tired of all that flying and soaring?

What then?

I remember many years ago, a lady prayed for me in a church service. She told me that I was like an eagle, however, I was an eagle that was scared and frightened to open my wings and soar high because of knock backs, wounding, and that sense of abandonment I just couldn't seem to shake. She told me that I had been given a gift, one that would see many people come to know Christ. A gift that needed me to shine bright, become brave and understand who I am and *Whose* I am. And yet, for this little eaglet to fulfill her purpose, I needed to open my wings, believe God has indeed got me and called me for a purpose. So, I decided, if ever so slowly, to trust Him, open my wings and learn how to not only fly, but to *SOAR*.

Why tell me this now, Wendy?

Why wait until now to share this story?

Well, dear warrior, soaring is a special kind of flight path, it's different to gliding. Gliding sends you in a downwards direction whereas soaring is where the bird flies up into a rising air current,[10] and even though you know that you have a follow-up shot to aim at the enemy, sometimes, it's not that warriors don't believe that God cannot part waves, or rescue us from the enemy, but the truth of the matter is, we struggle to believe in ourselves. To have enough confidence to rise out of the ashes, open our dark red wings and soar high above anything we ever dreamed or imagined we could do for God's glory and His honour is for someone else and not for us. Right? We've had the 'tall poppy' syndrome pushed so far down into our broken souls, that any thoughts where we believe we can indeed rise above our circumstances are dowsed out by others who think we've become way too big for those warrior boots we've been wearing. The boots that have the dust and dirt from trampling on snakes and vipers, those shoes filled with God's peace that each one of His warriors have shod their feet with, to stand firm and strong when we have done everything else God told us to do on the battlefield. This is when others sit up and take notice. They suddenly start to become interested in what you're doing, what you're thinking, and why you feel like you can soar to the heights you know God needs you to go.

So, what do you do? You look at their folded arms and feel the stares digging into your dreams and you shrink back. And like me, you start to close those magnificent Phoenix wings, not showing others how majestic the dark red plumage of your feathers are, just in case they get jealous of your calling as you start to rise up from the version of yourself they believed you should be. And that song you've been singing, the one that you have sung with a confident expectation, the story and testimony of everything God had rescued and redeemed you from? Well, that suddenly becomes quieter and quieter because you've been warned to tone that song down, less is more you know. Better still, perhaps it's for the best if you just kept a lid on that passion that makes you come alive, okay? You're making the rest of us look bad.

Oh yes, you will now be on their radar, dear firebird.

For what it's worth, let me give you one piece of advice before you close this book and test out those wings of yours. God didn't take Himself to the agony of the cross and bear the scars of our sins just for us to be so humble that we'd never feel we'd be able to rise up and move from our insufficiency and soar high toward an all-sufficient God.

That's pride.

Remember, there is no more hiding, dear warrior!

So, how do you soar high and not get all tangled up in the nets that are thrown over your wings to trap and trick you into staying small? How do you find the strength to continue to rise higher into the promises and purposes God has for your life?

You wait.

Isaiah 40:28-31 teaches all firebird's how to soar.

>'Have you not known?
>Have you not heard?
>The everlasting God, the Lord,
>the Creator of the ends of the earth,
>neither faints nor is weary.
>His understanding is unsearchable.
>He gives power to the weak,
>And to those who have no might He increases strength.
>Even the youths shall faint and be weary,
>And young men shall utterly fall,
>But those who wait on the Lord,
>Shall renew their strength;
>They shall mount up with wings like eagles,
>They shall run and not be weary,
>They shall walk and not faint.' (NKJV)

That's the secret all firebirds who soar high have learned. To *wait on God* and not go flying off in their own strength. So, dear firebird, confidently open up those beautiful dark red majestic wings of yours for others to see how good God is. Soar high into the warm thermals of God's love and grace as you rise from the ashes of your past and fly high with the One who loves you so fiercely. And don't you ever forget what Miriam, the prophetess, worship leader and all-round great woman of God taught you, dear warrior...

'Sing to the Lord, all the earth; proclaim the good news of His salvation from day to day, declare His glory among the nations, His wonders among all peoples. For the Lord is great and greatly to be praised.' 1 Chronicles 16:23-25 (NKJV)

Pack your tambourine, dear warrior, it's time to raise a Hallelujah!

ACKNOWLEDGEMENTS

Transforming is a process, and to believe the process of taking a message from idea to book solely rested on the shoulders of the author, well, that would be a work of fiction resembling the mythical tale of the Phoenix. This list of people are the ones behind the scenes whose names do not get to grace the cover of this book; however, this does not make the part they played in its production any less important. As my mother used to say, 'The most important people are always the last to be acknowledged when they roll the credits.'

So, let's roll credits.

Omega Writers. Thank you for all your encouragement and prayers over the years in helping me find my 'voice' in my messages.

My sisters in Christ. Warriors are not made in peaceful times; they are shaped by life's battles. Keep rising, my friends. Keep rising.

Mum and Dad. Your songs help me to never question or doubt that God is indeed a Rescuer and a Deliverer. Thank you for your ongoing support in my writing.

Hazel Fanstone. My big sister. Although we cannot go on our regular bike rides anymore due to fact we live 10,566 miles apart, you still know your little sister loves you.

Elizabeth Chapman. Witnessing how Jesus took the ashes from your past and made them into something beautiful makes this G-Mama's heart sing! Thank you for the countless hours of selfless commitment so this message could reach others. 'Looking forward to the time we cannot count anymore.'

My husband, Philip. All the things that have tried to keep you colouring within the lines never did stand a chance of succeeding, for you follow Jesus, the box-breaker.

My children, Samuel, and Lauren. Forever thankful and proud to be called your mother. I love you both deeply and uniquely.

And finally, Yahweh. The One who has delivered me from the ashes of my past and invited me to trust Him completely in my rising. Learning what it truly means to *abide* in You gives me the courage to open my wings and soar.

www.ingramcontent.com/pod-product-compliance
Lightning Source LLC
Chambersburg PA
CBHW071957290426
44109CB00018B/2054